from the Schlipfs
4-14-06

The Baker
Book of
Bible
Travels
For Kids

The Baker Book of Bible Travels for Kids

Published in Grand Rapids, Michigan by Baker Book House.

ISBN 0-8010-4423-5

Printed in the United States of America.

1 2 3 4 5 6 7 — 02 01 00 99

The Baker
Book of
Bible
Travels
For Kids

Anne Adams

Published in
association with

BAKER
A DIVISION OF
Baker Book House Co

How to use the Baker Book of Bible Travels

This is a book about some of the more fascinating places in the Bible, about the people who traveled there, and about the exciting events that happened in these places.

In the Baker Book of Bible Travels you will find an **itinerary** which gives the Scripture where both the **traveler** and **destination** are mentioned in the Bible. The **topography** describes where the place was located and sometimes what it looked like. **Transportation** lets you know just that—if the traveler journeyed to the place by foot, ship, chariot or by another means.

As if this weren't enough, the **what to take** section lists some of the important people or things that the traveler needed on his journey, and the **reason for visit** tells you why the traveler went there in the first place! Read the **things to do** and **then and now** sections and you will learn exciting facts about the traveler's journey, the history of the place, and what's going on in that place today! I've also included the **date of arrival** so you know when in history the event took place.

As you read about each journey, try to imagine you are there! Feel the dust beneath the feet of Paul as he travels one hundred miles north through a dangerous mountain pass to reach Pisidian Antioch. I hope the events and characters of the Bible come alive for you, as they did for me!

Happy Travels!

Anne Adams

Contents:

Antioch (an-tee-ok)

Itinerary: Acts 11:25-26

Traveler: (Joseph) Barnabas, a follower of Jesus and a Christian leader

Destination: Antioch

Topography: Antioch was located in Syria on the river Orontes, about 16 miles from the Great Sea. Its nearness to the sea, as well as the fact that many caravan routes passed through the city, made it an important center for business.

Transportation: probably foot

What to Take: food and water

Arrival: between A.D. 46 and 47

Reason for Visit: When the new church in Antioch began to grow, Barnabas was sent from Jerusalem to help guide the new Christians. He soon realized that

he needed help. He went to Tarsus to find his good friend Paul and bring him to Antioch. Together they stayed for more than a year helping the church and teaching new believers about Jesus. It was the first church whose members were mostly Gentiles rather than Jews.

Things to Do: "Antioch the Beautiful and the Golden," as it was called, was already famous for its grand architecture which included a theater, a public bath, a basilica (law court), and a two-mile long street lined with columns and street lamps. When Rome conquered Syria in 64 B.C. and Antioch became the eastern capital of the Roman Empire, the Romans added to the beauty of the city by building palaces and temples, extending aqueducts and paving the main roads in marble.

Then and Now: Antioch was built in 301 B.C. by Seleucus Nicator. It is considered the greatest of 16 different Antiochs which he built in honor of his father Antiochus.

By the first century A.D., Antioch was a large city in the Roman empire with a population of about 500,000. Only Rome and Alexandria were larger. It was considered the center of Christianity outside Palestine, and it was here that believers of Jesus Christ were

Mediterranean Sea   Antioch

first called *Christians*. Paul and his companions were sent by the church in Antioch on his three missionary journeys. During the next 13 centuries, Antioch was conquered by the Arabs, Byzantines, Turks, Crusaders and Egyptians. It was struck by many earthquakes, including the one in A.D. 526 which killed nearly 250,000 of its people.

Today, the city of Antakya, the capital of the Hatay Province in southern Turkey, is a modest trade center. The agricultural plains which surround the city produce citrus fruit, grapes, olives, melons, wheat and cotton. Most of its original grandeur is gone, and only portions of the ancient city's walls, catacombs and aqueducts remain. The Antakya Museum contains a preserved collection of mosaics which date from the second and third centuries. The Castle of Antioch towers high above the modern city. It offers views of the Grotto of St. Peter, the cave church where the apostle once preached, as well as the Iron Gate, one of the original entrances to the biblical city.

Ashdod (ash-dod)

Itinerary: 1 Samuel 5:1–6:15

Traveler: The Philistines

Destination: Ashdod

Topography: The city of Ashdod was located three miles inland from the Great Sea on the southern coastal plain. It was on the Via Maris trade route, ten miles north of its sister city, Ashkelon. Its port by the sea was called Ashdod Yam, which means "Ashdod by the Sea," and served as an important coastal trading center.

Transportation: foot and iron chariots

What to Take: the Ark of the Covenant

Arrival: 1060 B.C.

Reason for Visit: When the Philistines defeated the Israelites and killed about 4,000 men, the Israelites moved the Ark of the Covenant from the Most Holy Place in the tabernacle into their camp for good luck. The Philistines learned what they had done, and they were afraid. "A god has come into the camp," they cried. "We're in trouble!" They promptly marched into

battle, defeated Israel soundly and captured the sacred Ark. They brought it to Ashdod and put it in the temple of their pagan god Dagon. On the first morning, their statue of Dagon had fallen to the ground, and on the second morning, its face and hands had been cut off. The people of Ashdod grew sick and rats infested their city. Wherever the Philistines moved the Ark, the people grew tumors and became ill. Finally, they had enough, and they returned the Ark of the Covenant to the Israelites.

Things to Do: The Philistines wanted to know if the God of the Hebrews was the source of their troubles. Two cows who had just given birth were hitched to a cart carrying the Ark and sent toward Beth Shemesh where the Israelites were waiting. Only a supernatural force could make the cows walk away from their nursing calves. When the animals did, the Philistines were forced to acknowledge the existence of God.

Then and Now: Ashdod was the Greco-Roman name for the city of Azotus. It was one of the Philistine's five chief cities and according to Hebrew tradition, was originally inhabited by giants called Anakim. It was an important religious center for the Philistines who worshiped many pagan gods. A shrine was built to honor Dagon, their chief god who was a powerful warrior figure, whom they believed sent rain and bountiful harvests.

Excavations of the Philistine city uncovered a clay statue in the shape of a throne. It was a goddess whom the excavators named "Ashdoda."

The Philistines were the Israelites' major enemy. Although Ashdod was assigned to the tribe of Judah, the Hebrews had difficulty driving the Philistines out because of their advanced weapons. The Israelites were still fighting with copper and bronze while the Philistines had learned to smelt iron. Israeli foot soldiers were no match against their enemies' iron chariots.

Israel's modern Ashdod or Eshdud was founded in 1956, just four miles from the ruins of the ancient city. According to Arab tradition, a hill called Givat Yona, the highest point in the city, is the place where a great fish spat out the prophet Jonah.

Ashkelon (ash-kuh-lon)

Itinerary: Judges 14:10-20

Traveler: Samson

Destination: Ashkelon

Topography: Ashkelon, a seaport on the Great Sea, was located in the Land of the Philistines in southern Canaan, about 12 miles northeast of Gaza. It was situated on the Via Maris trade route, also called the "Sea Road," which connected trade routes and sea lanes.

Transportation: foot

What to Take: The power of the Lord came upon Samson and gave him supernatural strength.

Arrival: 1120 B.C.

Reason for Visit: Samson was a judge in Israel with great strength. Although the Philistines and Israelites were enemies, he married a Philistine woman from Timnah. At the wedding feast he told a riddle to thirty Philistines. "If you give me the answer within seven days," he told them, "I will give you thirty linen garments and thirty sets of clothes. If you can't, you will give me the same." On the fourth day, the

Philistines threatened Samson's wife to reveal the answer to the riddle. She begged Samson for the answer and when he gave it to her, she told the men. When Samson discovered how the men figured out the answer to the riddle, he went to Ashkelon, killed 30 Philistines, stripped them of their clothes and offered them to the men.

Things to Do: Samson's father-in-law thought Samson probably hated his daughter for betraying him, so he gave Samson's wife to another man while Samson was in Ashkelon.

Then and Now: Ashkelon was one of the five main cities of the Philistines which included Ekron, Ashdod, Gaza and Gath, with each of the cities ruled by a "seren" or captain. They battled for centuries with the Tribes of Israel who settled in the mountain ranges east of the "Land of the Philistines."

It is believed Ashkelon could be over 5,000 years old, making it one of the oldest cities in history. It was destroyed so swiftly by the Babylonian army 2,400 years ago that archaeologists were able to uncover a city trapped between layers of dirt. Its strategic location by the coast prompted Phoenicians to rebuild it not long after. Later excavations dating to this time period revealed an unusual discovery—a graveyard for dogs. The skeletons of over 700 dogs were found, making it the largest dog cemetery in the

world. It is believed that dogs were considered sacred in Ashkelon and may have been used in local healing rituals.

Legend says Ashkelon may have been the birthplace of King Herod the Great. He built his summer state house in the ancient city, as well as palaces, baths, fountains and an aqueduct. Excavations have also uncovered a small bronze and silver calf, over 3,500 years old, which was kept in a shrine at the city's gate, and a marble statue of Nike, the Greek goddess of victory.

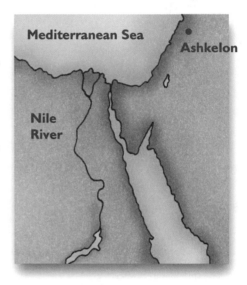

Modern Ashkelon, or Ashqelon, was resettled by Jews in about 1948 and is in southwestern Israel near Tel Aviv-Jaffa.

Athens (ath-enz)

Itinerary: Acts: 17:15-34

Traveler: Paul the apostle

Destination: Athens

Topography: Athens, the capital of the Greek state of Attica, was in the Roman province of Achaia and was named after its patron goddess Athene. It was about four miles from the Aegean Sea and was connected to its harbor by two walls. The city was built around a rocky hill called the Acropolis, the "Sacred Rock" of Athens.

Transportation: ship

What to Take: Paul carried to Athens his impressive knowledge of the Greek culture and language which helped him reason with the philosophers.

Arrival: A.D. 51

Reason for Visit: During Paul's second missionary journey, he fled from angry Jews in Berea who disapproved of his teachings. He sailed to Athens where he preached in the synagogue and the marketplace among Jews and Greeks. Some philosophers heard Paul's teachings and were curious. They invited him to explain his ideas at a meeting of the court called the Areopagus. Paul gave an

Athens

impressive sermon, and he reasoned with the Greeks on their own level, explaining why Jesus could be the only true God. Some sneered, but some came to know Jesus, including a member of the Areopagus!

Things to Do: Athens was a center of Greek culture, philosophy and education. They worshiped so many different gods that a Roman satirist once said, "It is easier to find a god at Athens than a man."

Then and Now: Under the leadership of Pericles in the 450s B.C., Athens became a city of high culture. Its population topped 200,000 at one point. Near the foot of the Acropolis was the Agora, a gathering place which was the heart of Athens. In this area, one could find administrative buildings, law courts, public services and temples. The people gathered here daily to buy and sell their goods, learn the news and discuss new ideas. Public announcements were even posted at the base of the statues in the "Eponymous Heroes Monument" in the Agora.

The Parthenon of the Acropolis, the ruins of which remain today, is considered the most important monument of ancient Greek civilization. It was a temple dedicated to the goddess Athena Parthenos and made almost entirely from marble. At one time it was home to the golden-ivory statue of Athena which stood over 10 meters high. Her right hand held an ivory statue of Nike, the goddess of Victory, and her removable dress and helmet were made of hammered plates of gold. The statue was lost during the first years of the Byzantine period. The lines of the Parthenon create an optical illusion so that the massive columns appear to curve slightly in the middle, giving the impression that they are bending beneath their weight.

Though the very first Olympic games of the ancient world took place in Olympia, Greece in 776 B.C., the first contemporary Olympic Games were begun in 1896 in Athens. Today, it is the capital of Greece and is the largest city in the country.

Visitors come from around the world to see the remains of the country's rich history. Near the Acropolis stands the Herodeion, an ancient theater erected in A.D. 161 by Tiberius Claudius Atticus Herodes. Originally called the Odeion, it was built to stage musical concerts to honor his wife who had died. The tradition continues each summer with the modern Athens Festival.

On the southern slope of the Acropolis are the ruins of the famous theater of Dionysos. Here, the plays of Aeschylus, Aristophanes, Euripides, and Sophocles - four of the greatest Greek dramatists - were performed. The National Archaeological Museum in Athens is called "To Museo" by the Greeks. Its collection of ancient artifacts is one of the largest in the country and includes the bronze statue of Poseidon, found just sixty-five years ago.

<u>Babylon</u> (bab-uh-lawn)

Itinerary: Daniel 1:1-6

Traveler: Daniel

Destination: Babylon

Topography: Babylon, "gate of God," was the capital of Babylonia in Central Mesopotamia. It sat on the Euphrates River, surrounded by a plantation of palm trees. An important caravan route connecting the Persian Gulf to the Great Sea passed through the city.

Transportation: foot

What to Take: Daniel was joined by thousands of Israelites, including his three friends, Hananiah, Mishael and Azariah.

Arrival: 605 B.C.

Reason for Visit: King Nebuchadnezzar of Babylon captured Judah and then laid siege to Jerusalem. He tore down the city walls and stole many sacred objects from the temple before he burned it down. He chose thousands of the most intelligent, well-bred and beautiful Israelites and brought them 500 miles to the city of Babylon. Daniel and his three friends were among the captives. When they arrived in their new home, they were given Babylonian names: Daniel was called Belteshazzar; Hananiah became Shadrach; Mishael became Meshach and Azariah became Abednego. The Israelites were held captive in Babylon for 70 years.

Things to Do: During Daniel's captivity, God worked miracles. Daniel interpreted dreams for the king, translated a prophetic message of God written on a wall at a royal banquet and was untouched when he was tossed into a den of lions. When Shadrach, Meshach and Abednego were thrown into a hot furnace, the son of God joined them, and they were not harmed!

Then and Now: Babylon was founded by Nimrod, the great-grandson of Noah. During the reign of King Nebuchadnezzar II, it became the political, cultural and religious center of the Babylonian Empire. It was a beautiful city which covered more than 200 square miles. Part of its defenses included an outside wall, a middle wall and an inner wall, all made of brick and over 300 feet high. A moat, 30 feet wide, surrounded the city. The Ishtar Gate was the most elaborate of eight bronze gates and was decorated with glazed blue brick and over 150 bulls and dragons.

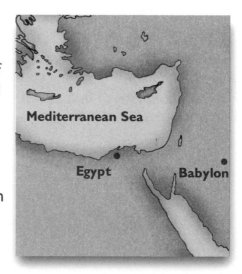

Mediterranean Sea

Egypt

Babylon

One of the king's greatest achievements was the Hanging Gardens of Babylon, one of the Seven Wonders of the Ancient World. The structure has been compared to an artificial mountain, 400 square feet and at least 80 feet high with raised terraces filled with trees and plants. It was watered by a chain pump which lowered buckets into the Euphrates and delivered the water to the top.

Today, the ancient city lies in ruins 56 miles south of Baghdad in the modern country of Iraq. Excavations at the site uncovered the remains of a ziggurat, a temple in the shape of a stepped pyramid which was once seven stories tall. It is believed to be part of the famous Tower of Babel. An inscription by Nebuchadnezzar II was found on the temple tower which read in part, " I have completed its magnificence with silver, gold. . . Since a remote time, people had abandoned it, without order expressing their words."

In 700 B.C. the prophet Isaiah foretold of the destruction of Babylon and said the city would never be inhabited again. Since the city's demise in about 300 B.C. to the present day, Babylon has remained in ruins. The city became shrouded in superstition when Alexander the Great tried to rebuild Babylon and then died. This and the fact that the soil around the city is no longer fertile has kept Arabs from camping and grazing their sheep here. The Baghdad Railway line passes within yards of what was once one of the most beautiful cities in the world.

Beersheba (bihr-shee-buh)

Itinerary: Genesis 21:8-14

Traveler: Hagar, mother of Ishmael

Destination: the desert of Beersheba

Topography: Beersheba was the city furthest south in the kingdom of Judah. The phrase "from Dan to Beersheba" was used when referring to the most northern and southern boundaries of the Promised Land. Beersheba was also the northern gateway to the Negev desert.

Transportation: foot

What to Take: food, a skin of water, and Hagar's son Ishmael

Arrival: about 1967 B.C.

Reason for Visit: Abram and his wife Sarai were very old when God promised Abram a son. Their faith was weak, and they doubted God. Sarai asked her young servant Hagar to become Abram's wife and bear him a child. Hagar did and she called her son, Ishmael. God renewed his promise to Abram and the covenant he had made with him. The covenant said

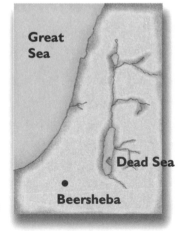

Beersheba

Abram, now called Abraham, would be the father of many nations.

When Abraham was 100 years old and Sarai, now called Sarah was 90, their son Isaac was born. Eventually, Sarah grew tired of Hagar and Ishmael. She told Abraham to get rid of them. The next morning, Abraham led Hagar and her son into the desert of Beersheba. God comforted them. Ishmael became the ancestor of the Arab nations just as Isaac is the ancestor of the Hebrew nation.

Things to Do: The desert surrounding Beersheba was desolate. In this southern region of Israel, trees were rarely found anywhere except on cultivated farms. Still, God provided Hagar and her son with shade and a well for water.

Then and Now: Beersheba was an oasis in a dry desert which received little annual rainfall. Its water supply came from underground streams which were tapped into by a cluster of wells. The name Beersheba, which means "well of the oath," was first given to a well dug by Abraham. It was by this well that Abraham and Abimelech, king of the Gerar region, made a peace treaty which allowed each other and their future offspring to live together peacefully. It became home to Isaac and Jacob and was one of the cities given to the tribe of Simeon.

The modern town of Beersheba or Beer Sheva, is slightly southwest of the old city. There is an archaeological dig just outside of the city called "Tel Sheva" which is the site of Beersheba during the reign of King Solomon. Arabs still call the city Bir es-Seba meaning "well of the seven" because of the two large wells and five smaller ones which are still there.

Today the population of Beersheba includes local bedouins (nomadic Arabs), Israelis, Ethiopians, and Russians. The city has a thriving cultural center with many museums, a symphony and historical monuments which pay tribute to its long and interesting history. Beersheba is also home to Israel's famous Ben Gurion University.

Bethany (beth-uh-nee)

Itinerary: John 11:1-20

Traveler: Jesus

Destination: Bethany

Topography: The village of Bethany, "house of dates," was on the eastern slope of the Mount of Olives, two miles from Jerusalem. It was situated on the road to Jericho and was once described as a remarkably beautiful place, full of palm trees and very peaceful.

Transportation: foot

What to Take: Jesus took his disciples with him to Bethany.

Arrival: A.D. 31

Reason for Visit: When Jesus was preaching in the villages beyond the Jordan River, word came to him that his friend Lazarus, the brother of Mary and Martha, was very sick. Jesus stayed where he was for two more days and then went with the disciples to Bethany. By the time Jesus arrived, Lazarus had been dead for four days.

Martha was very upset and told Jesus, "Lord, if you had been here, my brother would not have died."

Jesus told her, "I am the resurrection and the life. He who believes in me will live, even though he dies; and whoever lives and believes in me will never die."

Jesus commanded them to take the stone away from the tomb, and he called in a loud voice, "Lazarus, come out!" Lazarus walked out of the cave, still covered in his grave clothes! On this day, many Jews put their faith in Jesus.

Things to Do: Bodies were wrapped in special grave clothes made of long strips of linen and then covered with fragrant plants such as aloe and myrrh. They were placed in tombs which were usually caves carved in the limestone hillsides whose entrances were sealed with large rocks. All burial sites were required to be outside of the city gates or limits. It was customary for families to hire at least one professional mourner to help them display their grief in public. The wealthier the family, the more mourners they were able to hire.

Then and Now: Bethany was a suburb of Jerusalem. Jesus spent much time here in the company of his close friends, Mary, Martha, and Lazarus. He also attended a feast at the home of Simon the

Leper. It was near Bethany, on the Mount of Olives, that Jesus began his Triumphal Entry into Jerusalem, and it was from this same vicinity that he ascended into heaven.

The modern town of Bethany, known today as Azariyeh, was built around the traditional site of the tomb of Lazarus. Dozens of steps descend steeply to the sacred tomb, now the property of Muslims who primarily inhabit the town. Since the end of the fourth century, pilgrims have been gathering at the tomb and in the fields around the town to worship on the Saturday before Palm Sunday.

The only other remains of the ancient town which overlooks the Jordan Valley, is a tower whose massive stones predate the Crusades. The Bethany Church of Lazarus was built to commemorate the raising of Lazarus from the dead. A beautiful mosaic in the church depicts the miracle.

Bethesda (buh-thez-duh)

Itinerary: John 5:1-2

Traveler: Jesus

Destination: Bethesda

Topography: Bethesda, "house of mercy," was a spring-fed pool or reservoir commonly referred to as the "pool of Bethesda" or sometimes "the sheep pool." It was located north of the Temple Mount in Jerusalem, close to the Sheep Gate or market.

Transportation: foot

What to Take: compassion

Arrival: 30-31 A.D.

Reason for Visit: While Jesus was in Jerusalem for a feast of the Jews, he visited the pool of Bethesda on the Sabbath. People who were blind, disabled or paralyzed would lie beneath the covered porches on mats. From time to time, an angel of the Lord would come and stir up the water. The first one to step into the pool after the water was stirred was healed of his infirmity. Jesus met a man there who hadn't walked for 38 years. He asked him, "Do you want to get well?" The man replied, "I have no one to help me get into the pool when the water is stirred. While I am trying to get in, someone else goes down ahead of me."

Jesus said to him, "Get up! Pick up your mat and walk." The man was instantly cured, and he picked up his mat and walked.

Things to Do: The Pharisees believed that doing any kind of work on the Sabbath was unlawful. When they heard that Jesus had performed a miracle and a man had carried his mat on this day, they accused him of breaking the law. Jesus told them, "My Father is always at his work to this very day, and I, too, am working."

Then and Now: The pool of Bethesda and other reservoirs, cisterns or tanks were vital to the survival of Jerusalem and were designed to supply the city with water. The rivers in Palestine were mostly small and often dry in the summer months. Rain water was very important as it filled the springs and fountains which in turn flowed into the storage tanks. Unfortunately, the water couldn't be stored for very long because it became dirty and unhealthy. In addition, there was little or no rain in the summer months, and water was often rationed.

Bethesda's pool was actually two masonry pools adjoined together. The northern pool was dug first during the reign of

Solomon, and the southern pool was added in the beginning of the second century B.C. It was fed by an underground spring and when the spring flowed, the water in the pool bubbled.

Solomon was very adept at water conservation. He made pools to water his forest nursery and dug and built the "Pools of Solomon" which were capable of holding three million gallons of water in a space of about seven acres.

The site of the original pool of Bethesda has always been debated. Some thought it was the modern "Fountain of the Virgin" in the valley of the Kidron. Other wells in the area were also believed to be the actual pool, but no evidence was found until around the last century.

St. Anne's Church in northeast Jerusalem was erected in the twelfth century over the site of a water reservoir. It was built on the wall which divided the reservoir's two pools. In 1888 when the church was undergoing repairs, the large reservoir was rediscovered. It was 55 feet long, 12 feet wide and had steep stairs which descended into it. A faded fresco on one wall, which depicted an angel stirring the water, led many to believe they had found the actual pool of Bethesda.

Bethlehem (beth-luh-hem)

Itinerary: Matthew 2:1-12

Traveler: The Magi

Destination: Bethlehem of Judea

Topography: Bethlehem, which means "house of bread" in Hebrew and Aramaic, was located five miles southwest of Jerusalem in the hilly country of Judea. It was about 2,550 feet above sea level and surrounded by shepherds' fields. The town was on the main highway to Hebron and Egypt and was called "Bethlehem of Judea" to differentiate it from another Bethlehem further north.

Transportation: camel

What to Take: The Magi or wise men carried gifts to Jesus to celebrate his birth. They brought gold (to symbolize virtue), frankincense (to symbolize prayer), and myrrh (to symbolize suffering).

Arrival: 5 B.C.

Reason for Visit: When wise men from the east looked into the sky, they saw the star of Jesus and knew the Messiah was born. They traveled to Jerusalem and asked his whereabouts so they could go and worship him. When Herod learned of this, he was disturbed. He was

afraid that the child called "the King of Jews" would someday take his throne. He called for the Magi and told them to go to Bethlehem of Judea, find the child and tell him where he was. The Magi followed the star until it stopped over the place where Jesus was. They went to him, worshiped him and gave him their gifts. They were warned in a dream not to return to Herod, so they traveled to their homes by a different route.

Things to Do: Bethlehem was the birthplace of David and the place where he was anointed by Samuel as the next king of Israel. It was from the well in Bethlehem that three of David's men brought him water when he was hiding from Saul in the cave of Adullam. It was also here that Jacob's wife Rachel died and was buried.

Then and Now: Bethlehem of Judea was also called Ephrath, Bethlehem Ephratah, and "the city of David."

The Church of the Nativity, one of the oldest churches in the world, was built over the traditional site of the "holy crypt," the cave or grotto where Jesus was born. It was built around 330 A.D. by Queen Helena, mother of the Roman Emperor Constantine the

Great. A marble altar filled with oil lamps and incense burners was built in the crypt.

The Latin scholar Jerome was said to have spent thirty years in this cave, translating the Bible into Latin.

The entrance to the Greek Orthodox section of this church is called "The Gate of Humility." Its door is only three and a half feet high and all who wish to enter must be willing to crouch low. It was built this size by Crusaders who once controlled the city, in an effort to stop Muslim horsemen from using the church as a stable.

Today, modern Bethlehem is located in the volatile West Bank, an area controlled by Israel since the end of the Six Day War in 1967. The Palestinian Authority has, however, been governing it since December 21, 1995. It is one of the few cities in the West Bank crowded with visitors from all over the world. Holy sites, like Rachel's Tomb, are guarded by soldiers to allow Jewish people to worship freely.

Bethsaida (beth-say-duh)

Itinerary: Matthew 14:13-21

Traveler: Jesus

Destination: Bethsaida

Topography: Bethsaida was a fishing village on the northeast shores of the Sea of Galilee near the site where the Jordan River flowed into the lake. It was situated on a prosperous trade route between Mesopotamia and Egypt.

Transportation: fishing boat

What to Take: Jesus' disciples went to him.

Arrival: A.D. 30

Reason for Visit: When John the Baptist was beheaded, the disciples buried his body and told Jesus of his death. Jesus climbed into a boat and withdrew to a private place, near Bethsaida. A large crowd was waiting for him, and Jesus felt compassion for them and healed their sick.

When dusk approached, the disciples went to Jesus and told him to send the crowds away so the people could go into the villages to buy food. "You feed them," Jesus told his disciples. The disciples only had five loaves of bread and two fish. Jesus took the food, looked to the Heavens, gave thanks, and then broke the bread. When the disciples passed out the food to the crowd of over 5,000, everyone ate, and there was plenty of leftovers!

Things to Do: After this amazing miracle, Jesus sent the disciples to the other side of the lake while he dismissed the crowd. He went up on a mountainside to pray and when he was through, Jesus walked on the water to reach his disciples in the boat.

Then and Now: Bethsaida was the birthplace of the apostles Peter and Andrew and was home to the apostle Philip. It was one of nine cities which populated the banks of the Sea of Galilee. When Philip Herod, son of Herod the Great, ruled the area in the first century, he rebuilt the town and renamed it Bethsaida Julius. Then, sometime during the Roman Wars between about 67-70 A.D., it was destroyed along with many other cities in the Galilee region. Unlike Capernaum, Chorazin and others, it was not rebuilt.

After the first century, Bethsaida was abandoned and was considered "lost." For nearly 2,000 years crusaders and travelers attempted to find the city but could not agree on its whereabouts. In the 1980's a Benedictine monk and archaeologist, Father Bargil

Pixner, began his search for the city. Looking through Scriptures and other historical records for clues, he determined that the ancient city was located at a mound called et-Tell, two miles from the Sea of Galilee—which in modern times served as a burial place for local Bedouins. Experts confirmed his suspicions that the Sea of Galilee had receded in size and concluded that Bethsaida was once located on its shores.

Excavations, ongoing since 1987, have uncovered an Iron Age palace, a temple, and a Bronze Age city wall. It is now believed Bethsaida may have been established around the time of the Egyptian pyramids and played a significant role during the time of King David.

Beth Shan (beth shawn)

Itinerary: 1 Samuel: 31:1-10

Traveler: King Saul

Destination: Beth Shan

Topography: The city of Beth Shan, "house of rest," was located on the eastern slopes of Mount Gilboa, overlooking the Jordan Valley. It was in the territory of Manasseh, 14 miles south of the Sea of Galilee. Beth Shan was a well-watered, fertile region making it an important station for caravans.

Transportation: Saul's body may have been transported on a cart.

What to Take: Saul was accompanied by the bodies of three of his sons: Jonathan, Abinadab and Malki-Shua.

Arrival: 1010 B.C.

Reason for Visit: When the Israelites met the Philistines on the slopes of Mount Gilboa, even their leader King Saul was afraid. The Israelites fled and many were slain, including three of Saul's sons. Archers overtook the king, and he was wounded critically. Saul knew that if he were taken captive, he would probably be tortured by the Philistines. "Draw your sword and run me through," he said to his armor-bearer. When the man refused, terrified, Saul drew his own sword and killed himself.

When the Philistines found the king, they beheaded him and stripped off his armor. Saul and his sons were brought to the town of Beth Shan where the king's head was placed in the temple of Dagon and his armor in the temple of the Ashtoreths. His body and those of his sons were hung on the walls of the city.

Things to Do: The Philistines placed Saul's armor in the temple of Ashtoreth, the goddess of fertility, to give her credit for the king's defeat. David later recovered the bones of Saul and his sons and buried them.

Then and Now: Beth Shan, later called Scythopolis by the Romans, was believed to be as old as 3500 B.C. It was the capital of

the Decapolis, a confederation of ten self-governing towns in the Roman Empire, and it was the only city in the alliance located west of the Jordan River.

The remains of Beth Shan are in Israel on a mound called Tell el-Husn, "Mound of the Fortress," near the Arab village of Beisan.

Beth Shan

Excavations have revealed 18 different levels of debris and ruins which means that the city was repeatedly destroyed and rebuilt. The ancient town was destroyed at one point between 1050 and 1000 B.C., the approximate time of King David. Many have speculated as to whether David himself, Saul's successor and Jonathan's friend, laid waste to Beth Shan.

Four Canaanite temples were unearthed at the site, one identified with the temple of the Ashtoreths and another with the temple of Dagon. One of the most impressive discoveries of Beth Shan is the Greco-Roman style amphitheater which may have seated up to 8,000 spectators. The stage was in a building two stories high and connected by spiral staircases which led to balconies. A ground area between the stage and the seats was used by the chorus. Circular, bone-colored tokens, found at the site, were believed used as theater tickets. Public streets, bath houses, Roman merchant shops, and temple and monument inscriptions by three pharaohs were also found among the ruins. A hippodrome, a large stadium used for chariot racing and theater performances, was uncovered on the outskirts of the city. It is currently being restored. Archaeologists say that when excavations of Beth Shan are complete, it will be one of the most spectacular Roman cities to be reconstructed in the Middle East.

Caesarea (sess-uh-ree-uh)

Itinerary: Acts 23:12-35

Traveler: Paul the apostle

Destination: Caesarea

Topography: Caesarea was also called Caesarea Maritima to distinguish it from Caesarea Philippi in Northern Israel. The city and its large harbor were located in Judea on the shore of the Great Sea, about 70 miles northwest of Jerusalem. Caesarea was also on the roadway between Tyre and Egypt.

Transportation: foot

What to Take: For Paul's protection, foot soldiers accompanied him from Jerusalem to Antipatris, and the cavalry accompanied him the rest of the way to Caesarea.

Arrival: A.D. 40

Reason for Visit: When Paul was in Jerusalem at the end of his third missionary journey, the Jews became very angry with his teachings and plotted to kill him several times. There was an uproar in the city, and Paul was seized and arrested. When Paul announced that he was a Roman citizen and wanted his case to be heard by

Caesarea

Caesar in Rome, the commander had no choice but to release him into protective custody of the governor of Judea. In the night, Paul began his journey to Caesarea under the protection of the Roman army.

Things to Do: Paul was forced to spend two years in Caesarea under house arrest. Eventually, he managed to speak to King Herod Agrippa II. He won favor with him, and Paul was finally allowed to sail to Rome.

Then and Now: The foundations of a huge temple dating to the end of the first century B.C. were uncovered in 1995. It was believed to be about seven stories high, surrounded by columns and capped at its ends by triangular gables—making it similar in appearance to the Greek Parthenon. Its impressive height and location near the sea made it a beacon to guide ancient mariners to the harbor.

Excavations also revealed a hippodrome used to stage chariot races and a Roman stadium where Israelites were thrown to wild beasts in punishment for their revolt against the Roman Empire.

Today, Caesarea is a modern resort town on the Mediterranean coast in Israel. The ruins of the ancient city are the site of continual excavations.

Caesarea Philippi (sess-uh-ree-uh fil-i-pye)

Itinerary: Matthew 16:13-28

Traveler: The 12 disciples

Destination: Caesarea Philippi

Topography: Caesarea Philippi was located at the extreme northern boundary of Palestine, 120 miles north of Jerusalem and 20 miles north of the Sea of Galilee. The city was on the southern slopes of Mount Hermon near a large spring, the upper source of the Jordan River. The area was known for its beauty and tranquility.

Transportation: foot

What to Take: The disciples accompanied Jesus.

Arrival: A.D. 31

Reason for Visit: Jesus led his disciples from Bethsaida to the region of Caesarea Philippi. When they were gathered around him, he asked, "Who do people say the Son of Man is?" The disciples replied that some thought it was John the Baptist, Elijah, Jeremiah or one of the prophets. Simon Peter spoke up and said, "You are the Christ, the Son of the Living God." Jesus was very pleased with him because he knew that Peter's answer was revealed to him by God. He warned the disciples not to tell his true identity to the rest of the world until God's timing was in place. Jesus spoke to them about the establishment of the church and of Peter's important role in it. He also told them that it was necessary for him to suffer, die and be resurrected in order to save mankind.

Things to Do: Jesus told the disciples, "If anyone would come after me, he must deny himself and take up his cross and follow me." He meant that people must be willing to risk their lives for him now and receive their reward later.

In Roman times, the common form of execution was crucifixion. The condemned were forced to carry their crosses through the streets to the execution site.

Then and Now: Caesarea Philippi was in a prime location because it was continuously watered by the runoff from Mount Hermon. The area was originally called Paneas since the cave beside the springs was associated with the Roman nature god Pan. During the first century, Herod the Great built a temple here. His son, Herod Philip, then founded a city. He named it "Caesarea" to honor Emperor Caesar Augustus and "Philippi" to honor himself and to distinguish it from Caesarea on the coast. Later, Herod Agrippa II rebuilt the city and enlarged it to cover several hundred acres. It became one of the largest and most splendid cities in Palestine. He renamed it Neronias in honor of Emperor Nero, and it served as his capital for almost half a century.

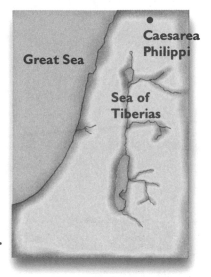

Excavations on the city began in about 1988 and revealed part of a structure believed to be an Asclepium, an ancient healing center. It was built on five levels or terraces and was about 100 meters wide, making it one of the largest structures of its kind ever discovered. A colonnaded main street still awaits excavation.

Today, the city is known as Banias and is in the Golan Heights section of Syria, occupied by Israel since 1967.

<u>Cana</u> (kay-nuh)

Itinerary: John 2:1-11

Traveler: Jesus

Destination: Cana of Galilee

Topography: Cana was a town in the highlands of Galilee, near Capernaum and west of the Sea of Galilee. It was called Cana of Galilee to distinguish it from another town, Cana of Asher.

Transportation: foot

What to Take: Andrew, Peter, Philip and Nathanael, the first disciples, traveled to Cana with Jesus.

Arrival: A.D. 29

Reason for Visit: Jesus, his mother Mary and his disciples were invited to a wedding in Cana. While there, Mary mentioned to Jesus that there was no more wine to serve the guests. Jesus told the servants to take six jars used for ceremonial washing and fill them with water. Then he told them to draw some of the water and serve it to the master of the banquet. When the master tasted it, the water had already turned into wine. He declared it to be the best wine ever. This was the first of Jesus' many miracles, and it helped his new disciples to put their faith in him.

Things to Do: On another of Jesus' visits to Cana of Galilee, he performed his second miracle. When a royal official heard that Jesus was in Cana, he traveled from Capernaum and asked Jesus to please come and heal his son. Jesus didn't need to go with the man in order to perform the miracle. He told the man to return home because his son would live. The man believed. On his way home, his servants met him and told him that his son was healed. It happened at the exact hour which Jesus spoke the words to him.

Then and Now: While Cana of Galilee was very significant because it was the place where Jesus performed his first two miracles, little else is known about it. It was the home of Nathanael, one of Jesus' first disciples, and it is mentioned four times in the Scriptures, all in the book of John.

Some people believe the ruins of the ancient city are at the modern site of Khirbet Kana, eight or nine miles from

Nazareth. Many more, however, think it likely that Cana once stood at modern Kefr Kenna, a rural area northeast of Nazareth which is on a direct road to the Sea of Galilee.

In 1641 Franciscan monks tried to acquire access to this site which they believed was the biblical Cana. After two hundred years, they finally succeeded and in 1881 a Franciscan church was built over the site where Jesus was thought to have changed the water into wine. Inside the church there is a shrine upon which sits a large water jar, representative of one used at the time. The Saint Nathanael Church was resurrected over the site where it is believed the disciple Nathanael was born.

Today, Cana or Kefr Kenna is a village of Christians and Moslem Arabs. It is a beautiful place which is dotted with country homes and surrounded by cactus, pomegranate, and olive trees. Churches of different denominations have sprung up including Orthodox, Melkite, Latin, and Baptist.

The Greek Orthodox Church is in possession of two large vases of stone which they believe are two of the six waterpots used at the wedding which Jesus attended. Other findings at the site include the remains of a Christian tomb, an ancient church, a synagogue, and a silo for grain.

Capernaum (kuh-pur-nuhm)

Itinerary: Luke 4:31-37

Traveler: Jesus

Destination: Capernaum

Topography: Capernaum was a town in Galilee located on the northwestern shore of the Sea of Galilee. It was a busy fishing port and a toll collecting station on the great highway from Damascus to Acco and Tyre on the Great Sea.

Transportation: foot

What to Take: Everywhere Jesus went, the power of the Spirit of God went with him.

Arrival: A.D. 29

Reason for Visit: Although Jesus was raised in Nazareth, his

teachings were not accepted by many of the people there. He left and went to Capernaum where he performed many great miracles and gave wonderous teachings. One Sunday, while teaching in a synagogue, a demon-possessed man called out to Jesus. Jesus told the demon to be quiet and commanded him to leave the man. Immediately, the demon threw the man down and left, and the man was not hurt. The people were amazed, and the news of what Jesus had done spread throughout the area.

Things to Do: Capernaum was a city of great wealth but low moral character. Jesus chose this city as the center for his ministry. He was allowed to teach in the synagogues because it was customary for visitors to speak on the Sabbath. Since Capernaum was the headquarters for many Roman troops, word of his teachings spread throughout the Roman Empire.

Then and Now: It is believed Capernaum was home to three of Jesus' first disciples—Andrew, Matthew and Peter. While some of Jesus' greatest miracles were performed here, the people remained sinful. In the Gospels of Matthew and Luke, Jesus warned of the destruction of the city if the people did not repent. The prophecy was fulfilled because at some point in history Capernaum disappeared.

Most believe that the ruins of Capernaum are located at modern Tell Hum in Israel. Although the ancient city was large, little of its remains have been found. A beautiful synagogue and altar, built between the second and fourth centuries and later restored by Franciscan monks, was built over what appears to be the remains of the original synagogue where Jesus taught. Beside it are the remnants of a "house church," thought to have been constructed over the site of the apostle Peter's house. Jesus often stayed here when he was in Capernaum, and it also served as a meeting place for Christians.

An excavated street, portions of walls made of black basalt and mortared with mud and pebbles, appear to form the residential section of an ancient town. The only other traces of a once bustling city are the olive presses, found in a grove of olive trees next to the remains of the synagogue. Many of the presses, used to crush the fruit in order to extract the oil, were found intact.

Colosse (kuh-lah-see)

Itinerary: Colossians 4:7-9

Traveler: Tychicus, the apostle Paul's helper

Destination: Colosse

Topography: The city of Colosse was located on the Lycus River in the region of Greater Phrygia in Asia Minor, 100 miles east of Ephesus. It sat on the most important trade route from Ephesus to the Euphrates River and served as a trading center.

Transportation: foot

What to Take: Tychicus carried Paul's letter to the Colossians.

Arrival: A.D. 62

Reason for Visit: While Paul was in Ephesus during his third missionary journey, he sent his friend Epaphras to Colosse to establish a church there. Paul knew Epaphras had the heart of a pastor because of how much he loved God and prayed for believers. Epaphras later visited Paul while he was under house arrest in Rome and brought him disturbing news about the church. False teachers

were leading the believers to worship angels instead of God and telling them that knowledge or philosophy was more important than faith. Paul immediately wrote a letter to the Colossians in which he presented the truth and encouraged them to act like Christ in every part of their lives. Tychicus, Paul's close friend, delivered Paul's letter to the church.

Things to Do: The church at Colosse met in the home of Philemon, an important citizen. On Tychicus' journey to Colosse, he was accompanied by Onesimus, a runaway slave who was returning to his owner Philemon. He carried a personal letter.

Paul wrote to Philemon, encouraging him to welcome the slave back. Tychicus also delivered Paul's letter to the Ephesians. All three letters are books of the New Testament.

Then and Now: For more than 1,000 years, from 500 B.C. to A.D. 600, Colosse was an important city. It had a large Jewish population which formed when Jews fled persecution in Jerusalem under the rule of Antiochus III and IV. Greeks and others were also drawn to the city because it was on a major trade route. The interesting mix of cultures brought new ideas and religions.

Colosse

Eventually, Colosse became a center of Oriental mysticism. The city was renowned for an unusual purple wool and a glossy black wool, both of which were used to make cloaks and carpets.

The region of Phrygia of which Colosse was a part, is probably best known for the legendary King Midas who ruled Phrygia from 738 through 695 B.C. His skeleton was found on a large bench in a burial chamber 20 feet long and 17 feet high. More than 166 bronze funeral gifts were also found on the floor of the tomb. Greek mythology tells the story of the king who desired that everything he touched be turned to gold. When Dionysus, the god of wine, granted his wish, Midas came to regret his choice when even his food and water were changed to gold. Biblical Colosse was destroyed by the Turks in the twelfth century. Modern Chonas or Chonum in Turkey is located near the ruins of an ancient church.

Corinth (kor-inth)

Itinerary: Acts 18:1-17

Name: Paul the apostle

Destination: Corinth

Topography: Corinth was a city in the ancient Roman province of Achaia. It was on the southern tip of the isthmus which connected the mainland to the peninsula. It was a great commercial center due to its strategic location. All land traffic from the north of Achaia to the south passed through the isthmus and Corinth. Its eastern and western ports also offered direct access between the Adriatic and Aegean Seas.

Goods were often shuttled through the city between the ports by way of a wooden railway.

Transportation: foot

What to Take: Paul carried the materials he needed to use in his trade as a tentmaker.

Corinth

Arrival: about A.D. 51

Reason for Visit: During Paul's second missionary journey, he traveled from Athens to Corinth and stayed with his new friends Aquila and Priscilla. He preached in synagogues on the Sabbath, but many Jews didn't like his message. The Lord spoke to Paul in a vision and told him not to be afraid and to continue to speak the Word of God.

Soon after, the Jews brought Paul to court claiming that he was persuading them to worship God in unlawful ways. Gallio, the leader of Achaia, dismissed their charges and made them leave the courtroom. Paul stayed in Corinth for a year and a half.

Things to Do: When Paul was in Corinth, he earned his keep by working as a tentmaker, a trade he learned as a boy. He established one of his largest churches here and wrote to the church on two occasions. These letters, found in the New Testament, are the books of First and Second Corinthians.

The city was wealthy, luxurious, and wicked. Its many cults were given to the worshiping of pagan gods such as Poseidon, the god of the sea. A temple to Aphrodite, the goddess of love and war, was built on a large hill, 2000 feet high, called the Acrocorinthus.

Then and Now: Ancient Corinth was thriving as one of the greatest commercial centers of all times until the Romans invaded

Greece in 146 B.C. General Lucious Mummius destroyed nearly the entire city, brought its art treasures back to Rome as spoil and sold the survivors into slavery. Corinth was in ruins for nearly a century until Julius Caesar reestablished it as a Roman colony. By 7 B.C. it was one of the earliest cities, next to Aegina, to strike and use coins called "silver starters." By A.D. 27, while Athens was the educational center of Achaia, Corinth was considered the commercial and political center. Its biennial Isthmian Games were second only to the Olympic games of Athens.

In 1858 a severe earthquake destroyed much of ancient Corinth and left ruins spread over six acres which are visible today. A new city was built several miles away and it too, was destroyed by an earthquake in 1928. It was rebuilt and is the city known today as modern Corinth in southern Greece.

Crete (kreet)

Itinerary: Titus 1:5-9; 3:12

Traveler: Paul the apostle

Destination: Crete

Topography: Crete, an island in the Great Sea, formed a natural bridge between Europe and Asia Minor. Its mountainous regions were filled with chestnut, oak and cypress forests and parts of the coastal areas were tropical with sandy beaches and palm trees. The northern coast provided several good harbors, but the southern side of the island had steep cliffs unsuitable for shipping.

Transportation: cargo or grain ship

What to Take: Paul traveled to Crete with Titus, his friend and helper.

Arrival: between A.D. 62 and 65

Reason for Visit: When Paul was released from prison in Rome at the end of his third missionary journey, it is believed that he and Titus traveled together for a while.

They went to Crete and when it was time for Paul to leave, he asked Titus to stay and minister to the churches there. After Paul left, he wrote a letter to Titus asking his friend to appoint elders in every town and to sharply rebuke those who were liars and deceivers. When Titus had finished his work in Crete, he was to meet Paul in Nicopolis where the apostle was wintering before his final imprisonment under Emperor Nero.

Things to Do: It is believed that Crete may have been a training center for Roman soldiers. This would have contributed to its pagan influence. In addition, its strong roots in mythology and the worship of other gods made the islanders lacking in true godliness. Titus had his work cut out for him when Paul wrote to him that "Cretans are always liars, evil brutes, lazy gluttons." (Titus 1:12)

Then and Now: Human life on the island of Crete can be traced as far back as the sixth millenium B.C. during the Neolithic period and through the rise and fall of the Minoan civilization. Crete was also part of the flourishing Bronze Age and once boasted of having "a hundred cities." Greek mythology with its many legends says that

King Minos, one of the three sons of Zeus, ruled the island for a long time from his palace in the city of Knossos.

The island's strategic location between the Great Sea and the Aegean Sea and its nearness to Africa and Asia Minor made it attractive to other nations. Crete was invaded and conquered numerous times. In 1913 it was ceded to Greece, but in 1941 Germans conquered the Greek mainland and launched an airborne invasion of Crete. They occupied the island for four years until it was freed by British forces in 1945.

Crete has long been respected as a cultural center where painting and literature flourished. It was home to the famed painter El Greco who produced beautiful portraits of the Virgin and Christ, as well as the Cretan writer Nikos Kazantzakis who wrote the famous book "Zorba the Greek" while on the island.

Today, Crete is the largest island in Greece and the fifth largest island in the Mediterranean, separating the Aegean from the Libyan Sea. It is home to many important archaeological sites, including the remains of the most luxurious Minoan palace in Knossos.

Cyprus (sye-pruhss)

Itinerary: Acts 13:4-12

Traveler: Saul and Barnabas

Destination: Cyprus

Topography: Cyprus was an island in the eastern portion of the Great Sea, west of Syria and south of Cilicia. It was about 3,500 square miles with mountains to the north and south. Mount Olympus at 6,406 ft. was its highest peak. A flat, treeless plain ran from the western coast to the east.

Transportation: cargo ship

What to Take: John Mark accompanied Saul and Barnabas to help them.

Arrival: A.D. 46

Reason for Visit: Saul and Barnabas visited Cyprus on their first missionary journey. When they arrived in the town of Paphos, the

governor of the island called for them because he wanted to hear about God. While the missionaries talked to him, the governor's private sorcerer argued with them about the Word of God. Saul, who was now called Paul for the first time, told the sorcerer that

because of his deceit and trickery, he would become blind for a time. When the magician was struck blind, the governor was amazed. He knew

that Paul and Barnabas were telling the truth about God.

Things to Do: Since the island of Crete was home to Barnabas, the missionaries believed this would be a friendly place to begin their first journey. They landed in Salamis first, the largest city, where they preached in the Jewish synagogues before traveling across the island to Paphos.

Then and Now: The history of Cyprus, interesting and mysterious, is filled with ancient legends. Its roots are tied to Greek mythology where it is said that Aphrodite, the goddess of love and beauty arose from the waves of the Great Sea near the shores of Paphos in 800 B.C.

The island has long been famous for its folk art. In the ancient Greek epic poem *The Iliad*, by Homer, a beautiful breastplate was sent as a gift to King Agamemnon from the island of Cyprus. In

Antioch

Cyprus

Mediterranean Sea

addition, the famous sword of Alexander the Great was said to have been made here. Handmade embroidery, known as OLefkaritikaO, is named after the village from which it originated. Legend has it that Leonardo Da Vinci found an embroidered tablecloth so exquisite, he brought it back with him and placed it on the altar of the Milan Cathedral.

Cyprus, once inhabited by many including the Phoenicians, Greeks, Romans, Turks, and British has been an independent country since 1960. It is the third largest island in the Mediterranean today and a major center of tourism with over a million visitors every year. It is known as a stepping stone to three continents because of its nearness to Africa, Asia and Europe. Its fertile plains and cool mountains produce carob, olives, citrus, bananas, grapes and potatoes. The island is strewn with churches, monasteries, castles and palaces which date to the Byzantine period and the days of the Crusaders.

Damascus (duh-mas-kuhss)

Itinerary: Acts 9:1-25

Name: Saul of Tarsus

Destination: Damascus

Topography: Damascus, a city in Syria, was west of Mt. Hermon and about 150 miles north of Jerusalem. It was watered by the Abana and Pharpar rivers and was famous for its beautiful gardens, orchards and olive groves. Caravan routes from the east, west and south met in Damascus carrying silk, perfumes, carpets and food.

Transportation: foot

What to Take: Saul carried letters from the high priest in Jerusalem to the synagogues in Damascus. These letters were intended to help him take the Christians back to Jerusalem as prisoners.

Arrival: A.D. 35

Reason for Visit: Saul, born in Tarsus, was a devout Jew and an outspoken leader in the persecution of Christians. On the road to Damascus, where he intended to round up more believers, he was thrown to the ground by a dazzling light from heaven. The Lord asked Saul why he was persecuting him and told him to continue to Damascus where he would be told what to do. The light blinded Saul for three days. When God sent the disciple Ananias to lay hands on him, Saul's vision was restored and he was filled with the

Holy Spirit. It wasn't until later, during his first missionary journey, that Saul became known as the Apostle Paul.

Things to Do: Immediately, Saul began to preach in the synagogues of Damascus. The people were angry. They surrounded the city and guarded the gates. Saul escaped when he was lowered in a basket through an opening in the wall.

Then and Now: A famous saying says, "The world began at Damascus, and the world will end there." This refers to the fact that Damascus is one of the world's oldest continuously inhabited cities and has flourished for more than 40 centuries.

Today, Damascus is the capital of Syria and the chief center of commerce, located between Jerusalem and Beirut. Its elevation is a pleasant 2,000 feet, and it sits beside the modern Barada River which continues to water its famous orchards of apricots, almonds, figs and quince. Damascus was famed for its merchandise of beautiful craftsmanship. Damask, a type of patterned fabric, was named after the silk fabrics woven there. Workshops in the Old City still make Damask silk brocade, gold and silver filigree jewelry, carpets, inlaid woodwork and copper and brass goods. The city also produces the famous Steel of the Ancients, an extremely hard steel used in knives and swords. Each piece of steel is unique and resembles the pattern of the damask cloth.

The huge seventh century Omayyad Mosque is very ornate. Inside, a silver sepulchre holds what is said to be the severed head of John the Baptist. All of the streets of Damascus are crooked and narrow except for the "street called Straight," where Saul stayed during his visit here. It is the main road and is known today as "Queen's Street."

Dothan (doh-thuhn)

Itinerary: Genesis 37:12-17

Traveler: Joseph, son of Jacob

Destination: Dothan

Topography: Dothan, "two wells," was located 13 miles north of Shechem, midway between the Great Sea and the Jordan River. It was surrounded on the north, east and south by the hills of Samaria in the fertile Dothan Valley and lay along a major trade route to Egypt.

Transportation: foot

What to Take: Joseph wore the colorful robe given to him by his father Jacob.

Arrival: 1733 B.C.

Reason for Visit: Jacob sent his youngest son, 17-year-old Joseph, to check on his brothers who were tending sheep in the fields. When Joseph approached the area of Dothan, he was spotted by his brothers. "Here comes the dreamer!" they said. They were jealous because they knew Joseph was Jacob's

favorite son. "Come now, let's kill him and throw him into one of these cisterns and say that a ferocious animal devoured him." Reuben, Joseph's oldest brother prevented his brothers from killing Joseph.

They stripped Joseph of his beautiful robe and threw him into a dry well. When Reuben was away, they sold him as a slave to a caravan of merchants heading to Egypt. They dipped his robe in goat's blood and brought it to Jacob who believed a wild beast had killed his beloved son. He refused to be comforted and mourned the death of Joseph.

Things to Do: Joseph traveled for 30 days through the desert to Egypt, probably chained and on foot. He was sold to Potiphar, a rich officer in Pharaoh's service. He worked on the first floor of an elaborate home that had gardens, balconies, golden tableware and hand carved chairs. God had his hands on Joseph, and eventually he became the ruler of Egypt under Pharaoh.

Then and Now: Ancient Dothan was inhabited as early 3000 B.C. At the time of Joseph, it had a well-built fortress and a thick wall which sat on one of many hills in the region of Samaria. It had always been of strategic importance being the eastern-most of the three main passes between the Sharon Plain and the Jezreel Valley through the mountainous ridge of the hill country. It was near an important caravan route upon which traders from the east carried luxury goods such as spices, medicine and cosmetics to the wealthy in Egypt.

Nearly a millennium after Joseph was sold into slavery here, the prophet Elisha took up residence in Dothan. When the king of Aram found out that Elisha was revealing his battle plans to the king of Israel, he sent his army to Dothan and surrounded the city. Elisha's servant was afraid, but God opened his eyes and he saw the hill around the city filled with heavenly horses and chariots of fire.

Today, ruins of the ancient city are in a mound called Tell Dothan. It sits on a large hill which rises above the surrounding valley. The eastern and southern slopes are covered with olive groves and watered by a spring on the south side of the tell. This water source was probably the same one which watered biblical Dothan.

The two wells from which the city was named are still in existence. One is believed to be the cistern which Joseph was thrown into. It is called Jubb Yusuf or "pit of Joseph."

Emmaus (e-may-uhss)

Itinerary: Luke 24:13-35

Traveler: Cleopas, a disciple

Destination: Emmaus

Topography: The village of Emmaus, "warm wells," was about 60 stadia or 7 miles from Jerusalem, possibly to the northwest.

Transportation: foot

What to Take: Cleopas walked with another disciple.

Arrival: A.D. 33

Reason for Visit: On the day of Jesus' resurrection, Cleopas and his companion were walking on the road from Jerusalem to Emmaus. They were talking about what had happened that day. A stranger approached and walked beside them. "What are you discussing together as you walk along?" he asked.

Cleopas appeared sad when he told him about the death of Jesus of Nazareth, the visions of angels at the tomb, the rumors of his resurrection, and the disappearance of his body. "We had hoped that he was the one who was going to redeem Israel," he said.

When the stranger heard this, he became angry at their lack of faith and told them what the Scriptures said about the coming of the Messiah.

It was getting dark and Cleopas and his friend invited the man to stay with them. While the stranger sat at the table, he took bread, broke it, gave thanks and gave it to them. The instant the disciples realized the stranger was Jesus, he disappeared from sight.

Things to Do: Cleopas and his companion returned to Jerusalem and told the disciples, "It is true. The Lord has risen!" Jesus appeared to his followers many times before leading them to the vicinity of Bethany. He blessed them, then was taken up to Heaven. After his ascension, the disciples worshiped him and returned to Jerusalem.

Then and Now: The actual site of the village of Emmaus is not known for sure. We do know that according to ancient texts of Luke's gospel, Emmaus was 7 miles from Jerusalem. Many identify it with modern El Qubeibeh, the site of a Roman fort called Castellum Emmaus. A large church was built there in 1901 over the site of a Crusader's church dating to the 12th century.

Inside were found the remains of an ancient house thought to have belonged to Cleopas.

Some associate Emmaus with modern Amwas, called Nicopolis since the third century. It is the site of two lukewarm wells, a convincing piece of evidence since the Greek name Emmaus is based on a Semitic word meaning "warm wells."

Although it is about 20 miles from Jerusalem, seemingly too far, ancient texts of Luke's writing also give the distance to the ancient village as 160 stadia or 17 miles. These texts, however, are not considered reliable. Since the fourth century A.D., pilgrims to the Holy Land have considered Amwas the traditional site of Emmaus.

En Gedi (en-ged-ee)

Itinerary: 1 Samuel 24:1–25:1

Traveler: David

Destination: En Gedi

Topography: En Gedi, which means "fountain of the kid" in Hebrew, was an oasis on the western shore of the Salt Sea in the land of Judah. A natural fountain of water rising 600 feet above the sea created a lush, tropical habitat for plants, flowers and animals in the middle of the desert.

Transportation: foot

What to Take: David led an army of loyal men.

Arrival: about 1020 B.C.

Reason for Visit: King Saul was jealous of David and plotted to kill him. David fled to En Gedi where he fortified his army and kept watch. After David spared the king's life, here, he left and traveled into the Desert of Maon.

Things to Do: David and his men hid in the many caves, also called the "Crags of the Wild Goats." They probably bathed and refilled their water supply from the many pools of fresh water.

The caves of En Gedi, some large enough to hold 1,000 men, provided refuge for many armies. The area was in a strategic location, providing access to Judah, Jericho and the South. Caves were also used by local people for housing and tombs.

Then and Now: Today, En Gedi or Ein Gedi is still considered an oasis in the desert. In Israel, on the western shore of what is now the Dead Sea, its freshwater pools and waterfalls are enjoyed by those who visit the popular Ein Gedi Spa. Here, visitors take dips in the therapeutic salt water of the sea or in the area's natural hot sulfur springs.

A cruise boat called "Lot's Wife" offers excursions across the Dead Sea, below which are believed to be the remains of the ancient cities of Sodom and Gomorrah.

Ephesus (ef-uh-suhss)

Itinerary: Acts 19:1-41

Traveler: Paul the apostle

Destination: Ephesus

Topography: The city of Ephesus was on the River Cayster in Asia Minor, just a few miles from the Aegean Sea. It was a major trade center which connected the sea routes in the west to the land routes in the east.

Transportation: foot

What to Take: Aristarchus and Gaius accompanied Paul.

Arrival: A.D. 57

Reason for Visit: Paul returned to Ephesus on his third missionary journey, and God used him to perform extraordinary miracles. When Paul preached against the worship of false gods, a group of craftsmen led by the silversmith Demetrius started a riot. Many of the craftsmen were in the profitable business of making and selling silver

figurines of the goddess Artemis and other idols. They were afraid that Paul's teachings would hurt their trade and that they would lose money. The people shouted, "Great is Artemis of the Ephesians!" and they dragged Aristarchus and Gaius into the theater. The city clerk quieted the crowd, dismissing them, and Paul left for Macedonia.

Things to Do: Paul knew the Ephesians needed to hear God's Word. Many of them engaged in exorcism, black magic, and other occult practices. They worshiped many idols including Artemis, the goddess of fertility, and Dionysos, the god of wine.

Then and Now: During the first century A.D., Ephesus was the fourth largest city of the Roman Empire with a population of nearly 250,000. It was the capital and leading commercial center of the Roman province of Asia until its harbor filled with silt and it was eventually abandoned.

Following the crucifixion of Christ, it is believed that Jesus' mother left Jerusalem with the apostle John and lived in Ephesus until her death. Her restored home, The House of the Virgin Mary, is a site of pilgrimage for Christians today who visit modern

Ephesus in Turkey.

After John's exile on Patmos, he returned to Ephesus where he died several years later at the age of 104. The Basilica of St. John was built over his tomb.

Spectacular remains of the city were uncovered beginning in 1863. The Temple of Artemis, once considered one of the Seven Wonders of the Ancient World, was nearly a football field in length and four times the size of Athens' Parthenon. It had more than 100 columns over 55 feet high. The front wall of the Library of Celcus is all that remains of a building which once contained over 12,000 hand-written books, one of the largest collections of the ancient world. Outside the library was The Arcadian Way, called "the most splendid street of the Roman Empire." It was paved in solid marble, lined with columns and lighted with candle-like lamps. It led to the spectacular 25,000 seat theater where Paul gave sermons on occasion. The renovated Grand Theater hosts many theatrical performances today during the annual Efes Festival.

Ezion Geber (ez-ee-uhn gee-bur)

Itinerary: 1 Kings 9:26

Traveler: Solomon, third king of Israel

Destination: Ezion Geber

Topography: Ezion Geber, which means "the giant's backbone," was a seaport in the land of Edom on the Gulf of Aqaba. Cliffs, some as tall as 2,000 feet towered over the northern portion of this gulf which ran into the Red Sea. Coral reefs,  islands and sudden squalls made it a dangerous waterway for all but the sturdiest of ships.

Transportation: a "Tarshish ship" - a very sturdy ocean vessel which could navigate these difficult trade routes, built by Solomon.

What to Take: King Hiram of Tyre, Solomon's business partner, supplied Solomon's ships with his finest shipment and servants.

Arrival: around 940 B.C.

Reason for Visit: King Solomon, Israel's final king and the son of David, was wise, learned, and wealthy beyond measure. During his reign, he undertook a huge building program which included the original, most grand temple on Jerusalem's Mount Moriah. He also built his own elaborate palace. Entire cities were constructed to house his chariots and cavalry. Solomon used only the finest materials and became partners with King Hiram of Tyre who supplied him with the cedar and cypress wood used in the temple. Their partnership extended to the sea. Solomon decided to build a navy of ocean vessels and sail from Ezion Geber to Ophir, a region in Arabia rich in gold and precious stones. With Solomon's ships and Hiram's shipmen, the fleet successfully navigated the Gulf of Aqaba to Ophir and returned with much gold.

Things to Do: In addition to its value as a port on the Gulf of Aquaba, Ezion Geber was also a large copper and iron refinery. The local mines supplied the ore used in the smelters. Solomon was a wise businessman, and he must have made an investment here. It is said that the mines and the refinery were an important souce of his wealth.

Then and Now: The ancient town of Ezion Geber was the final resting place of the Israelites as they wandered through the wilderness to Kadesh. It was also here that Jehoshaphat built a fleet of ships similar to Solomon's with which to sail to Ophir. His were destroyed before

they left the port.

The city on the gulf was in a prime location for trade. Gold, silver, spices, and even men forced to work as laborers, arrived from Arabia. Ivory, gems, gold, monkeys and sandalwood came from Ophir. Most of these goods, in addition to the local copper, were carried north into Canaan on inland trade routes. Solomon even set up a prosperous trade monopoly at Ezion Geber, exchanging horses from Asia Minor for chariots in Egypt.

Today, the exact location of the ancient port is not known. It is believed that the Gulf of Aqaba once flowed ten miles further inland than it does today. If so, the site may be at modern day Tell Khelifeh where extensive excavations have taken place.

Gadara (gad-uh-ruh)

Itinerary: Matthew 8:28-34

Traveler: Jesus

Destination: Gadara

Topography: The town of Gadara was located on a steep hill southeast of the Sea of Galilee in the region of the Gadarenes. It was considered the best fortified city in the Roman province of Perea and also served as its capital. At the foot of the hill were thermal hot springs and baths.

Transportation: fishing boat

What to Take: The 12 disciples accompanied Jesus.

Arrival: A.D. 30

Reason for Visit: Jesus and his disciples crossed the Sea of Galilee into the region of the Gadarenes near the town of Gadara. When Jesus arrived, two demon-possessed men came to him from the tombs in the hills. They were violent and cried out to Jesus, "What do you want with us, Son of God?" The demons knew they would be cast out, and they begged Jesus to send them into a herd of pigs which were feeding nearby. Jesus said, "Go!" and the demons left the men and entered the pigs. The herd rushed over the steep cliff and fell into a lake where all the pigs drowned. When the townspeople heard about what happened, they were afraid of the supernatural power of Jesus and begged him to leave.

Things to Do: Jesus asked the demon his name, and it replied, "Legion, for we are many." A legion was the largest unit of the Roman army with 3,000 to 6,000 soldiers. The men were possessed by many demons, none of which could enter the herd of about 2,000 swine until Jesus gave his permission.

Then and Now: Gadara, a city comprised of mostly Gentiles, was one of ten cities which formed the Decapolis. Settled centuries earlier by Greek traders and immigrants, the cities banded together to form an alliance which offered them protection and increased trade opportunities in the region and around the world. Each of the cities, though part of the Roman Empire, was self-governed.

Gadara was a cultural town of artists, poets and philosophers. Built out of black basalt, it was perched on a mountain summit overlooking the Sea of Galilee and the Jordan Valley.

Today, Gadara is known as Umm Qays or Um Keis and is close to the Syrian border. It has only been partially excavated, but archaeologists are confident that further digging will reveal a major city. Already the ruins of three theatres have been uncovered as well as an aqueduct, a temple, a colonnaded street and a hypocaust or underground heating system.

The cliffs surrounding the city are filled with tombs sculpted from the limestone rock. Some are 20 feet square with chambers hollowed out for bodies. Like the two demon-possessed men which met Jesus on the hill in Gadara, people still dwell in the hill of tombs today. A nearby field is strewn with stone coffins and their lids.

Gaza (gah-zuh)

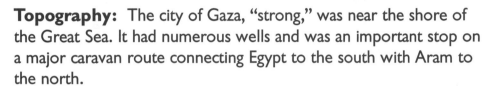

Itinerary: Judges 16:20-21

Traveler: Samson, an Israelite judge

Destination: Gaza

Topography: The city of Gaza, "strong," was near the shore of the Great Sea. It had numerous wells and was an important stop on a major caravan route connecting Egypt to the south with Aram to the north.

Transportation: Though Samson was now blind, he was probably forced to walk.

What to Take: The Philistines "accompanied" Samson.

Arrival: 1110 B.C.

Reason for Visit: When Samson fell in love with the Philistine woman Delilah, he revealed to her the source of his supernatural strength. She betrayed him and told his secret to the Philistines. When Samson slept, one of them cut off his seven braids, and he awoke to find his strength gone. Weakened, he was seized by the Philistines who gouged out his eyes and brought him to Gaza. Samson was thrown in prison, but his hair began to grow back. During a ceremony, he was brought to the temple of the pagan god Dagon and told to perform. He asked to be placed near the supporting pillars of the temple so he could lean against them. Then he prayed, "O God, please strengthen me just once more, and let

me with one blow get revenge on the Philistines for my two eyes."
He braced himself against the central pillars, his left hand on one, his
right hand on the other and cried out, "Let me die with the
Philistines!" He pushed with all his might and the temple fell, killing
thousands, including himself.

Things to Do: Samson was a Nazirite—an Israelite who devoted his
life to God and took a special vow. He was not permitted to cut his
hair, eat or drink any product made with grapes, including wine, or
touch a dead body.

Then and Now: Gaza is one of the oldest cities in the world. In
the fifteenth century B.C., the Egyptian king Thutmose III made it a
base for his army in a war against Syria. It was also the southernmost
of the five chief Philistine cities which included Ashkelon, Ashdod,
Gath and Ekron. Originally a seaport, it moved to a hill three miles
inland where it became the chief center of trade along the caravan
route to Egypt. It served the Nabatean nomads to the east whose
spice route passed through Petra, over the mountains of the Negev to
Gaza. In 1917, British forces during WWI seized the city from Turkey.

Today, modern Gaza or Ghazze is the principal city of the Gaza
Strip, a stretch of land 146 square miles. Occupied by Israeli forces
from 1967 to 1994, it is now the headquarters of the Palestinian
Authority. It is a conservative Muslim society where most women
wear the veil. Millstones, similar to the one used by Samson when he
was forced to grind corn in Gaza's prison, are still being used today.
The "hill of the watchman" or Tel el Muntar stands southeast of the
city and is the hill which Samson climbed, carrying the gates of ancient
Gaza which he had torn down.

Gibeon (gib-ee-uhn)

Itinerary: Joshua 10:9-10

Traveler: Joshua

Destination: Gibeon

Topography: Gibeon, "hill city," was an important Canaanite city, 15 miles northwest of Jerusalem and 20 miles west of Gilgal.

Transportation: foot

What to Take: The Israelite army

Arrival: 1210 B.C.

Reason for Visit: When Joshua and the Israelites conquered Ai in the land of Canaan, the people in nearby Gibeon became afraid for their safety. They knew the Israelites would not sign a peace treaty with the Canaanites, so they decided to trick Joshua. They went to the Israelites camp in Gilgal riding donkeys, wearing worn-

out clothes and carrying cracked wineskins and moldy bread. "We have come from a distant country," they said. "Make a treaty with us." Joshua and other leaders believed them and didn't consult God before signing a peace treaty with them. When Joshua learned that they were actually neighbors in the land of Canaan, he honored his oath, but he condemned them to be servants of Israel, woodcutters and water carriers, forever.

Things to Do: When five kings of southern Canaan found out that Gibeon had made peace with the Israelites, they joined forces and attacked the city. Gibeon called to Joshua for help, and Israel responded immediately. They marched all night from Gilgal and took their foes by surprise, driving them back through the Valley of Aijalon. During their fight, God sent huge hailstones from the sky, killing many Canaanites. He also made the sun and moon stand still for an entire day, giving Joshua more time in battle.

Then and Now: Gibeon was founded more than 3,500 years ago and was an important city in ancient Canaan, which lay within the territory of Benjamin. The tabernacle was kept in the city for several years after the destruction of Nob and before the temple in Jerusalem was built by Solomon.

It was in Gibeon that God appeared to Solomon in a dream and the king asked for wisdom to rule his kingdom. In the 7th century B.C., the city became wealthy from its production of wine, but it was finally destroyed by the Babylonians in 587 B.C.

Today, ruins of the ancient city are beneath the modern village of A-Jiib northwest of Jerusalem. Excavations unearthed 63 wine cellars, each capable of storing 42 large barrels of wine. Remains of a water system were also found including a large cistern known as the "pool of Gibeon." The pool, 36 feet in diameter, had 79 steps which descended to a depth of 30 feet. Blackened niches carved in the sides were used to hold the oil-lamps which lit the reservoir. It was beside this very pool that Abner of Israel and Joab of Judah each allowed 12 of their finest soldiers to engage in a one-on-one dagger match with the opposite side. When all of the soldiers were killed and neither side could claim victory, a full-scale battle ensued.

Golgotha (gohl-gah-thuh)

Itinerary John 19:16–20:18

Traveler: Jesus

Destination: Golgotha

Topography: Golgotha, "place of the skull," was the place where Jesus was crucified. Also known as Calvary, it was located in a garden just outside the gates of Jerusalem near the main highway.

Transportation: foot

What to Take: Jesus was forced to carry his own cross.

Arrival: 33 A.D.

Reason for Visit: Jesus was convicted of treason against Rome and sentenced to die by Pontius Pilate, the Roman governor of Judea. Though Pilate did not think Jesus committed a crime, the Jews would not allow him to free the Son of God. They shouted, "Crucify him! Anyone who claims to be a king opposes Caesar." Jesus was mocked, spit on, and flogged. Jesus was nailed to the very cross he carried to Golgotha and placed between two

prisoners who were also crucified that day. A placard was placed above his head upon which Pilate had written, "Jesus of Nazareth, the King of the Jews." Before Jesus died he murmured the words, "It is finished." He dropped his head and his Spirit left his body.

Things to Do: Joseph of Arimathea and Nicodemus took Jesus' body, prepared it for burial, and placed it in a new tomb near the spot where he was crucified. When Mary Magdalene and another

woman visited the tomb, there was a sudden earthquake. An angel appeared and rolled away the stone which sealed the entrance. Only the burial clothes of Jesus remained in the tomb. "Do not be afraid," the angel said, "he is not here; he is risen, just as he said." When the women ran to get the disciples, Jesus appeared to them and proved that it was true.

Then and Now: In 325 A.D., the Christian Emperor Constantine the Great sent his mother, Queen Helena, to Jerusalem to find the site of Golgotha. With the help of the Bishop Macarius, the site was identified as the spot where a Roman temple of Venus stood. Helena ordered the temple destroyed and a large portion of the earth carried away because she believed the soil was contaminated. During the digging, a tomb was unearthed as well as a Roman cistern filled with crosses and nails. A placard thought to be the one placed on the cross of Jesus was also found. Constantine's engineers cut away the surrounding cliff and built a large basilica, The Church of the

Golgotha

Holy Sepulchre, over the tomb and what they believed was the rock of Calvary.

Today, the church is located inside the walls of Old City Jerusalem. Controversy has arisen over the authenticity of the site because its location within the city walls contradicts the biblical account of Golgotha lying outside of the city gates. However, recent discoveries indicate that the original city's walls, since rebuilt in 1542, may not have always enclosed the basilica. Inside the church, the tomb or holy sepulchre, 6 feet wide, 7 feet long and over 7 feet high, is kept lit by 43 gold and silver lamps.

Hazor (hay-zor)

Itinerary: Joshua 11:1-11

Traveler: Joshua and the Israelite army

Destination: Hazor

Topography: The city of Hazor was located in the hills of northern Palestine. It was nine miles north of the Sea of Galilee and five miles west of the waters of Merom, a small lake through which the Jordan River flowed. Hazor was on  the main trade route between Mesopotamia and Egypt, making it an important trading center.

Transportation: foot

What to Take: bows and arrows, wooden shafted spears with bronze heads, curved swords and short axes

Arrival: 1200 B.C.

Reason for Visit: Joshua and the Israelites conquered the entire southern half of Canaan in one campaign. They killed many people in order to rid the land of sin. When King Jabin of Hazor found out what had taken place, he alerted the kings in northern Canaan as

Hazor

well as clans like the Amorites and the Hittites. They joined forces and camped at the waters of Meron to wait for Israel.

The Lord told Joshua, "Do not be afraid of them, because by this time tomorrow I will hand all of them over to Israel, slain." Joshua and the Israelites attacked the army of the northern kingdom and defeated them soundly. They made their horses lame and burned their chariots. Then Joshua turned back and captured Hazor, killed the king and burned the city.

Things to Do: Joshua and the Israelites went on to capture the rest of Canaan. The entire conquest of the Promised Land lasted seven years.

Then and Now: During the second millenium B.C., Hazor was the greatest city-state in Canaan. It covered an area of 200 acres, had a population of about 20,000 and was ten times the size of ancient Jerusalem. It was well defended with walls at least 50 feet high and a moat 50 feet deep and 260 feet wide. The city's size and strategic location on the trade route between Egypt and Babylon made it the

head of all the city-states in Canaan. When the Israelites destroyed Hazor, it was rebuilt in part by Kings David and Solomon, followed by Kings Ahab and Jeroboam II, but it never regained its former grandeur. It was abandoned sometime around the second century B.C.

Excavations on Tel Hazor in Israel were first conducted in 1928 and continue to the present day. Finds included four cuneiform tablets which may lead to the discovery of the royal archives, hundreds of pieces of coats of mail, the king's silver toga pin, an Egyptian battle ax, a dagger, arrowheads, and a ceremonial sickle-shaped sword worn by kings or generals. Evidence of the fire which destroyed the city was apparent in the thick layer of ash which covered remains of the royal palace. The fire was so hot, the mud brick walls turned glass-like. Flames were apparently fueled by the wooden floors and the large vats of cooking oil in the palace as well as the strong winds which whipped through the Hulah Valley to Hazor. Many of the treasures found in these ruins are on display in the Israel Museum in Jerusalem.

Hebron (hee-bruhn)

Itinerary: Genesis 13:1-18

Traveler: Abram

Destination: Hebron

Topography: The city of Hebron, also called Kirjath-arba, was located 19 miles southwest of Jerusalem and was on the main road to Beersheba. The hills surrounding the city grew fine grapes, and Hebron was known for the excellent wine it produced.

Transportation: foot

What to Take: Abram took his wife Sarai, his nephew Lot, and all of their possessions.

Arrival: 1990 B.C.

Reason for Visit: After God promised Abram the land of Canaan, he left Haran and traveled like a nomad from place to place, building altars to the Lord. When he was in the Negev, he realized that there was not enough land to sustain both his family

and Lots. He told his nephew that they must part company and gave him the first choice of land. When Lot chose the fertile plain of Jordan in the east, Abram took his family to live in the land of Canaan. The Lord told him that the land belonged to him and his descendants and that his offspring would be as numerous as the dust of the earth.

Abram pitched his tents in Hebron near the great oaks of Mamre and built an altar to the Lord there.

Things to Do: When Sarah was 127 years old, she died in Hebron. Abraham was greatly saddened and looked for a special place to bury her. He approached the Hittites and asked if he could buy the cave of Machpelah which belonged to Ephron. When Ephron heard what Abraham wanted, he offered to give him the cave as well as the field for free. Abraham refused and paid full price, 400 shekels of silver.

Then and Now: Hebron means "a friend of God" in Arabic—a name which was given to Abraham. It is one of the oldest cities in the world, and tradition says it was home to Adam. When David was king of Judah, he ruled from Hebron for seven years before moving the capital to Jerusalem when he became king of both Israel and

Judah in about 993 B.C.

Today, Hebron is located in the West Bank. Although it was incorporated into Jordan in 1948, it was seized by Israel during the Six-Day war in 1967. A few hundred Jewish Israelis settled into central Hebron amidst tens of thousands of Palestinians, and the tension between the two groups has not abated.

The Cave of Machpelah also known as the Tomb of the Patriarchs, contains the burial sites of Abraham and Sarah, Isaac and Rebekah, and Jacob and Leah. It is the second most holy site in Judaism, next to the Temple Mount in Jerusalem. A synagogue and mosque were built over the tomb. In 1862 the first European, the Prince of Wales, was permitted to enter the holy mosque.

In the Valley of Eshcol, about three miles north of Hebron, stands one of the largest oak trees in Israel. It is believed by some to be the ancient tree under which Abram pitched his tent. It has been named "Abraham's Oak."

<u>J</u>ericho (jer-uh-koh)

Itinerary: Joshua 5:13–6:25

Traveler: Joshua

Destination: Jericho

Topography: Jericho was called the "City of Palms" because of the abundance of date palm trees which grew there. Located in the land of Canaan north of the Salt Sea and west of the Jordan River, it was an oasis in the bleak Judean desert. It was also one of the lowest cities in the world, around 1,000 feet below sea level.

Transportation: foot

What to Take: Joshua led the Israelites, including the priests who carried the Ark of the Covenant, into the city.

Arrival: 1220 B.C.

Reason for Visit: Joshua became the new leader of the Israelites after the death of Moses. He led them across the Jordan River which marked the eastern boundary of the Promised Land and into Jericho. God told the Israelites to march behind seven priests, blowing ram's horns one time for six days. On the seventh day, they marched around the city seven times and the priests blew the horns and the Israelites shouted. The walls of Jericho collapsed, and God's people charged in and took the city.

Things to Do: The Canaanites who lived in Jericho were very sinful. When the Israelites took the city, God ordered Joshua to destroy nearly everything in it. All of the people, except Rahab and her family, who helped the Israelites, were killed. Silver, gold, bronze, and iron objects were kept for the Lord's treasury, and then the entire city was burned.

Then and Now: Jericho, one of the oldest cities in the world, dates to about 8000 B.C. It was in a prime location near the Jordan River and the spring of Elisha where the prophet purified the bitter waters with salt. Its nearness to a ford in the river enabled Jericho to control the trade routes from the East. It also prospered from a medicine which it extracted from balsam and then exported.

There are three Jerichos. Remains of the Old Testament city are believed to be at the site of Tel es-Sultan, near the ruins of the New Testament city and about one mile from the modern city. When archaeologist Dr. Kathleen Kenyon excavated the original site in the 1950s, she found the remnants of 23 cities, each rebuilt atop the previous one over a span of 8,000 years. She didn't find evidence of the walls of Joshua's Jericho, but believes they may have been eaten away by the elements of nature.

Over the years, Jericho declined and by the end of the nineteenth century, it was deserted. When archaeologists, historians and scholars from around the world began to converge on the site, the sheer amount of traffic in the area caused a new Jericho to begin to grow. In 1994 it became the first town in the West Bank to come under Palestinian administration. Just outside the modern city are the remains of Herod's winter palace and due west is the mountain believed to be the "Mount of Temptation," upon which Jesus was tempted by Satan in the Judean wilderness.

Jerusalem (juh-roo-suh-lem)

Itinerary: Mark 11:1-11

Traveler: Jesus

Destination: Jerusalem

Topography: Jerusalem, which means "city of peace," was often called Zion in the Old Testament. It was 33 miles east of the Great Sea, 14 miles west of the Salt Sea and high in the Judean hills, surrounded by deep valleys. It was not very large, only about one mile in length and five-eighths of a mile in width.

Transportation: donkey's colt

What to Take: Jesus rode with his 12 disciples near him.

Arrival: A.D. 33

Reason for Visit: Jesus and his disciples left the Mount of Olives for Jerusalem on the Sunday before his crucifixion. He sent two disciples into the next village to find a donkey's colt. When they brought it back, they placed their cloaks upon the colt's back before Jesus sat on it. Then, when the people saw him coming, they laid down cloaks and

branches on the road before him. As Jesus entered the gates of Jerusalem, the people waved palm branches and joyously shouted, "Hosanna!" His entrance became known as the "Triumphal Entry" and the day as "Palm Sunday."

Things to Do: When Jesus approached the city, he wept for Jerusalem. The Jewish leaders had rejected Jesus as their King. He knew that the nation of Israel would fall into the hands of its enemies as a result of its lack of faith and disobedience.

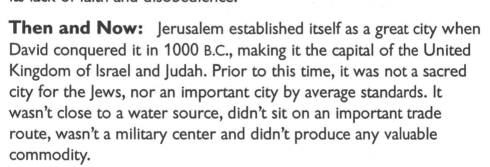

Then and Now: Jerusalem established itself as a great city when David conquered it in 1000 B.C., making it the capital of the United Kingdom of Israel and Judah. Prior to this time, it was not a sacred city for the Jews, nor an important city by average standards. It wasn't close to a water source, didn't sit on an important trade route, wasn't a military center and didn't produce any valuable commodity.

Today, Jerusalem is one of the most famous cities ever and of huge religious importance to Jews, Christians, and Muslims.

The modern city which sits on the same site as biblical Jerusalem is Israel's inland capital. The Old City is still surrounded by walls originally built by the Turks in the sixteenth century. Its seven functioning gates lead to separate quarters for Armenians, Christians,

Jerusalem

Jews and Muslims. The Western Wall in the Jewish quarter is the only visible remains of Herod's second temple, erected on the Temple Mount. It is the most holy site in Judaism.

The Temple Mount which sits atop Mount Moriah where Abraham went to sacrifice his son, is also home to the Muslim Dome of the Rock or the Mosque of Omar. This is the third holiest site in Islam after Mecca and Medina.

The Via Dolorosa which means "Way of Sorrows" is the route which retraces the steps of Jesus to his crucifixion. It begins on the northern side of the Temple Mount, runs through the Armenian and Arab quarters and finishes in the Church of the Holy Sepulcher, built upon the traditional site of Golgotha where Jesus was crucified.

Tradition says that Jesus made his Triumphal Entry into Jerusalem through the Eastern Gate and will return through this gate again. It is said the gate was sealed by Muslims when they occupied the city in an attempt to stop the Messiah from returning.

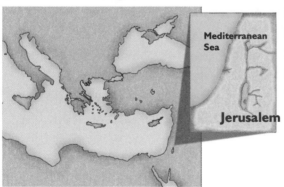

<u>Joppa</u> (jop-uh)

Itinerary: Acts 9:36-43; 10:9-23

Traveler: Peter the Apostle

Destination: Joppa

Topography: Joppa, which means "beauty" in Hebrew, was the chief seaport of Judea. It was located on cliffs 125 feet above the Great Sea, about 30 miles northwest of Jerusalem. It was one of Palestine's earliest ports and had a natural breakwater which protected its small harbor.

Transportation: foot

What to Take: faith

Arrival: A.D. 39

Reason for Visit: Peter was in Lydda when disciples came to him and asked him to come to Joppa. There, a kind woman named Tabitha (Dorcas) had died. Peter went to her, got down on his knees and prayed. Then he spoke to her and told her to get up. Tabitha opened her eyes and when she saw Peter, she sat up.

When news of this miracle spread throughout the city, many people came to know the Lord. Peter stayed in Joppa for a while and lived in the home of Simon the tanner.

Things to Do: While Peter was sitting on the housetop of Simon the tanner, he received a vision from God known as the "vision of tolerance."

Then and Now: It is said about Joppa that "scarcely has any other town been so often overthrown, sacked, pillaged, burned and rebuilt." Joppa was conquered by the Egyptians in about 1468 B.C. when it smuggled its soldiers through the ancient city's walls and other defenses in baskets. In the tenth century B.C., Solomon developed Joppa's harbor and it was through this port that cedar was shipped from Lebanon to Jerusalem for the construction of the Temple. Jonah also set sail from Joppa to Tarshish in an effort to escape God's command.

Today, Joppa is known by the name of Jaffa. Its neighbor, Tel Aviv, began as a suburb of the ancient city in 1909 when a group of Jews left the overcrowded Jaffa. They bought sand dunes north of the city and divided the property into parcels of land by drawing lots. Today, Tel Aviv is Israel's largest and most cosmopolitan city. It was adjoined to its mother town in 1950, and today the area is known as Tel Aviv-Jaffa.

It is a unique combination of culture and history. Jaffa's ancient waterfront still towers over the Mediterranean. The Arch of the Shofar which sits at the top of the city, commemorates the blowing of the horn around the walls of Jericho and St. Peter's Monastery pays tribute to the famous apostle.

A lighted, beach-front walkway lined with palms connects the old city to Tel Aviv where yachts rest by its shores. Some of Israel's most luxurious hotels and restaurants are here as well as the Israeli National Theater, the Israel Philharmonic, and the Tel Aviv Stock Exchange, Israel's only such institution.

Jordan River (jor-duhn riv-ur)

Itinerary: Matthew 3:1-17

Traveler: John the Baptist

Destination: the Jordan River

Topography: The name of the Jordan River was derived from a Hebrew word which means "the descender." The snows of Mount Hermon in northern Palestine fed four smaller rivers which joined to form the Jordan River proper. The Jordan then descended over 200 miles as it traveled south through the Sea of Galilee, the Great Rift Valley and to its final destination, the Salt Sea, where there was no outlet.

Transportation: foot

What to Take:
John was considered the forerunner of Jesus and a messenger of God. He carried and delivered a divine message when he prophesied of the coming of the Messiah.

Arrival: A.D. 29

Reason for Visit: John told people of the coming of the Messiah and warned them to repent. When the people came to him and confessed their sins, he baptized them in the Jordan River and they became spiritually clean.

One day Jesus came to him to be baptized, but John refused. He didn't feel worthy to baptize the Savior. Jesus insisted and when he arose from the water, the heavens opened. The Spirit of God descended upon Jesus like a dove and said, "This is My Son whom I love and with whom I am well pleased."

Things to Do: John was the first true prophet in over 400 years, and people were drawn to him because he was unusual. His garments were made of camel's hair and he wore a leather belt around his waist. He ate locusts and wild honey. People came to him from Jerusalem, Judea and all of Jordan. While he baptized them in water for repentance, he reminded them that the Messiah was coming to baptize them with the fire of the Holy Spirit.

Then and Now: The Jordan River marked the eastern boundary of the Promised Land. After the death of Moses, Joshua led the

Jordan River

Israelites across the river, which God rolled back, and into the land "flowing with milk and honey."

The Jordan, which has flowed for at least 3,500 years, was the largest river in Palestine. It is unusual that a large city was never built on its banks, and many have speculated as to why. The river was largely unsuitable for boats. Along its winding course from the Sea of Galilee to the Salt Sea were 27 rapids and many dangerous curves. It was swampy and shallow in parts and not very wide. In addition, there were a number of wild animals which roamed its banks.

Today, the source of the Jordan River is in eastern Lebanon and southwestern Syria. Its northern portion marks the boundaries between Israel and Syria and Israel and Jordan. The southern part is in Jordan, and the western part in Israel. Its fertile banks grow bananas, oranges, dates, mangoes, lemons, almonds and peaches. People come from around the world to renew their baptism or to bring precious drops of Jordan River water back to their loved ones.

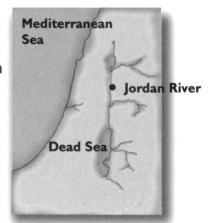

Lydda (lid-uh)

Itinerary: Acts 9:32-43

Traveler: Peter the apostle

Destination: Lydda

Topography: Lydda, also called Lod, was about 30 miles northwest of Jerusalem on the southern edge of the Plain of Sharon. It was located on the highway to Joppa called the "Valley of the Smiths" and near the major trade route between Egypt and Babylon. Due to its strategic location, it was a fairly successful commercial center.

Transportation: foot

What to Take: faith

Arrival: A.D. 39

Reason for Visit: While Peter was traveling through Judea, he stopped in the town of Lydda to visit the Christians. He met a man named Aeneas who was paralyzed and had been confined to his bed for eight years. Peter told him, "Aeneas, Jesus Christ heals you. Get up and take care of your mat." Immediately, Aeneas rose and walked.

When news of the miracle spread throughout Lydda and the region, many people came to know the Lord.

Things to Do: During Peter's tour of Judea, he was called to Joppa where he raised Tabitha, also called Dorcas, from the dead. While Peter was staying at the home of Simon the tanner, he received the "vision of tolerance." Through this vision, God showed Peter that Gentiles as well as Jews were worthy to receive Christ. Peter was then called to Caesarea where he ministered to a group of Gentiles—Cornelius the Centurion and his relatives and close friends.

Then and Now: Records of Lydda's existence, referred to as Lod in the Old Testament, date to the fifteenth century B.C. The city was built by Elpaal, fortified in the days of Joshua and destroyed and rebuilt several times through the centuries. During the first Jewish revolt from 66-70 A.D., it was razed by the Romans and later resettled and renamed Diospolis. Lydda was famous for its purple-dyed cloth, but renowned for stories of St. George, the patron saint of England who was martyred here.

George Adam Smith was serving in the Roman legion when he was converted to Christianity. Legends tell of a town terrorized by a dragon. When the king's daughter was about to be sacrificed to it, George Smith slaughtered the dragon, rescued the princess and converted the entire town to Christianity. Constantine the Great proclaimed St. George the "champion knight of Christendom." The principle order of knighthood in England was placed under the patronage of the saint. The Cross of St. George, a scarlet cross on a white background represents the Union Jack, the national flag of England. The legendary knight was martyred and buried in Lydda in 303 and a great church was erected over his tomb.

Today, ruins of the ancient city as well as the modern city known as Ludd are located in Israel.

<u>Malta</u> (mawl-tuh)

Itinerary: Acts 27:33–28:11

Traveler: Paul the Apostle

Destination: Malta

Topography: Malta, an island in the Great Sea, was located 60 miles south of Sicily. It was about 95 square miles, and in ancient times was called "Melita," a Phoenician word meaning "refuge." This was a fitting name since the island was often used as a haven for shipwrecked sailors. It had excellent harbors and was an ideal location for trade.

Transportation: Egyptian grain ship

What to Take: Luke accompanied Paul on this journey.

Arrival: about A.D. 59

Reason for Visit: Due to Paul's work with the Gentiles, he faced much persecution after he arrived in Jerusalem on his third missionary journey. He was placed in protective

custody to keep him from the Jews who wanted to hurt him. Paul was taken to Caesarea where he remained in prison for two years. Finally, he was allowed to sail to Rome where he could be tried as a Roman citizen.

Under the constant watch of Julius, a Roman centurion, Paul sailed for 14 days in hurricane strength winter winds. The ship was wrecked in a bay on the northeastern coast of Malta. All 276 passengers and crew were safe, but they spent three months on the island waiting until the end of the winter storm season.

Things to Do: Paul visited the home of Publius, the chief official of the island, and prayed for his sick father. After Paul laid hands on him, he was healed. When word of the miracle spread through the island, the sick came to Paul. They, too, were healed.

Then and Now: Malta's excellent natural harbor provided a shelter for naval fleets. Its location, considered the crossroads of the Great Sea, also made it an attractive island to conquering nations. If a nation controlled Malta, it controlled the shipping lanes along this sea route. It was colonized by the Phoenicians in about 1000 B.C. but was later conquered by many including the French and the British. During World War II, Malta was one of the staging areas for the U.S. Armed Forces invasion in Sicily. Malta became independent in 1964. Today, it is the largest island in the Maltese archipelago which includes five islands in all, three of which are inhabited. Its mysterious history includes Neolithic temples which, according to new research, are older than the famous pyramids of Giza in Egypt. The Hypogeum, a subterranean burial site, was found by accident in 1902. It descends three or more stories below to where the bones of over 7,000 people were found. This structure was believed to have been carved over several hundred years with the simple tools of flint and obsidian. Malta also has an impressive collection of museums which include the National Museum of Archaeology, the National Museum of Fine Arts and the Maritime Museum. Its economy is largely dependent upon ship-related industries such as the construction and repair of naval ships. Valetta, the island's capital, is home to the historic Grand Harbor, Malta's main seaport. It is considered one of the finest natural ports in all of Europe.

Megiddo (me-gid-oh)

Itinerary: 2 Chronicles 35:20-27

Traveler: Josiah, sixteenth king of Judah

Destination: Megiddo

Topography: Megiddo, "place of troops," was a hill city in northern Palestine which overlooked the Jezreel Valley. Its location enabled it to control two important trade routes—the Via Maris which linked Egypt in the south to Syria and Mesopotamia in the north and the road which connected eastern Palestine with the Great Sea.

Transportation: chariot

What to Take: King Josiah's troops and chariots of war

Arrival: 609 B.C.

Reason for Visit: After Babylon defeated Nineveh in 612 B.C., its empire grew stronger and threatened to dominate the ancient Middle East. Pharaoh Neco of Egypt gathered his troops and marched north through Judah to join the weakened Assyrians in war against Babylon. King Josiah didn't want Neco to pass through his land, so he prepared for battle. Quickly, Neco sent a message,

"What quarrel is there between you and me, O king of Judah? It is not you I am attacking at this time, but the nation with which I am at war. God has told me to hurry; so stop opposing God who is with me, or he will destroy you." Josiah didn't listen. He waited for Neco in the narrow pass which led to the plain of Megiddo, but archers were waiting for him. With a flurry of arrows, Josiah was badly wounded and died in a chariot on his return to Jerusalem.

Things to Do: Josiah was greatly loved in Judah and ruled from the age of 8 until his death at 39 years old. He was a godly king, and during his reign he rid the land of idols and renewed a covenant between God and the people.

Then and Now: Megiddo, originally one of the royal cities of the Canaanites was called the "queen of cities of Canaan and Israel." It was prosperous as a result of its location on two important trade routes, but the city saw no peace. Megiddo was considered a military prize because "the capture of Megiddo was the capture of a thousand towns."

From its beginnings in about 3000 B.C. until it was mysteriously abandoned in the fourth century B.C., the region which included the Valley of Jezreel was an area of continual violence and bloodshed. For those attackers who desired to reach Jerusalem, the way was often through the Valley of Megiddo known as the Valley of Decision.

Megiddo

The city was heavily fortified and had an impressive water system built by King Ahab. A tunnel extended from the top of the city's hill to a deep well outside. The well's original opening was sealed to prevent attackers from poisoning the source. Since water was always available and food was grown within the city, Megiddo could resist siege for a year or more. When Solomon fortified the city, he added a palace and the famous Stables of Solomon which housed about 450 horses and 600 chariots.

The significance of Megiddo is far from over. Though it lies in ruins in Israel, it is believed to be the site of the future Battle of Armageddon mentioned in the book of Revelation. Here, the army of evil will battle the army of God in the final showdown.

Mount Carmel (mount kar-muhl)

Itinerary: 1 Kings 18:15-40

Traveler: Elijah the prophet

Destination: Mount Carmel

Topography: Mount Carmel, about 1,790 feet high, was part of a range of mountains in Central Palestine which extended from the Plain of Jezreel northwest to the Great Sea. Carmel, which means "park" in Hebrew, was covered with lush flowers, shrubs, and herbs.

Transportation: foot

What to Take: Elijah wore his mantle or cloak

Arrival: 864 B.C.

Reason for Visit: When King Ahab and his wicked wife Jezebel ruled over Israel, they led the people to worship pagan gods, like Baal. The nation suffered a severe drought, and God told his prophet Elijah to present himself to Ahab. Elijah told the king to gather the prophets of Baal and the people of Israel on Mount Carmel.

When everyone was assembled,

117

Mount Carmel

Elijah challenged the false prophets in front of the Israelites. "We will both prepare a sacrifice," he told them, "but we will not set fire to it. You call upon the name of your god, and I will call upon the name of the Lord. The god who answers by fire—he is God."

All day long the prophets of Baal cried out to their god, but he didn't answer. Then, Elijah prayed to the Lord, and the sacrifice was consumed in flames. He killed the false prophets, and God sent rain to water the land.

Things to Do: When Jezebel learned that Elijah had slain the prophets, she sent word to him that he would be killed. Elijah feared for his life and ran to Beersheba where the angel of the Lord gave him food and water. He went to Mount Sinai, and God spoke to him in a gentle, comforting whisper.

Then and Now: The region of Carmel was coveted for many reasons. Its underwater springs provided water through a Roman aqueduct to cities like Caesarea. Mount Carmel was also considered a holy place to many religions. Shrines were built on its summit to

the pagan gods Carmel, Baal, and Zeus, and caves on its western slopes were home to many monks. Some of these caves, excavated for the first time in the 1920s, contained flint tools, animal bones and human burials dating back

500,000 years to the lower and Middle Paleolithic Ages.

Mount Carmel in northeastern Israel continues to be home to different religions. The Bahai religious faith chose Mount Carmel for its world headquarters and temple, and in 1150 the Carmelite religious order was founded. Its Stella Maris Church and monastery once served as a hospital site for Napoleon's soldiers. A monument to French soldiers was erected in front of the church.

Another Carmelite monastery, Muhraka, was built on the east end of the ridge where it is believed Elijah defeated Baal's prophets. Nearby, the traditional site of Elijah's cave where the prophet stayed, has become a pilgrimage center for Jews, Christians, Muslims and Druze.

Mount Hermon (mount hur-muhn)

Itinerary: Matthew 17:1-13

Traveler: Jesus

Destination: Mount Hermon

Topography: Mount Hermon, "Mountain of the Old Man," was part of a mountain range which marked the northern boundary of Palestine. It was about 40 miles north of the Sea of Galilee. The highest peak was 9,232 feet high and was usually always covered with snow. It was the highest landmark on the eastern coast of the Great Sea. Its three summits were called "the Hermonites."

Transportation: foot

What to Take: Peter, James and John, the brother of James, went with Jesus.

Arrival: A.D. 31

Reason for Visit: Jesus left Caesarea Philippi with three of his disciples and led them to a very high mountain, believed to be Mount

Hermon. When they were at the top, the face of Jesus became bright like the sun and his clothes became white like light. Then, Moses and Elijah suddenly appeared and talked with Jesus. A cloud enveloped the two prophets and Jesus, and a voice from within the cloud said, "This is my Son, whom I love; with him I am well pleased. Listen to him."

The disciples were terrified and fell to the ground, but Jesus came to them. He touched them and said, "Get up. Don't be afraid." Jesus told them not to tell anyone what they had seen until after his resurrection.

Things to Do: This miraculous event came to be known as the Transfiguration. It was a vision which offered the disciples a brief glimpse of the glory of God. Moses and Elijah were the two greatest prophets in the Old Testament. Moses represented the law or the old covenant and Elijah represented the prophets who foretold the coming of the Messiah.

Then and Now: The limestone ridge, of which Mount Hermon is a part, is about 20 miles long. Snow from its peaks melts and creates the runoff which continuously feeds the springs at its base. These springs form the headwater or source of the Jordan River. This range once formed a natural boundary for Herod's kingdom. All of his territories were south of the 9,232 foot summit.

Mount Hermon

Mount Hermon was also called "Jebel-et telj" or "Ice Mountain." Prior to the advent of refrigeration, its peaks provided the ice used by the resorts of Lebanon as well as Damascus. Caesarea Philippi was built on its southern slopes by Herod Phillip, son of Herod the Great. The mountain springs were an important source of water for the city which became the capital of Herod's kingdom for nearly half a century.

Today, Mount Hermon is part of the Anti-Lebanon mountain range. It lies partly in Syria and Lebanon and since the Six-Day War in 1967, a portion of it is in Israel's Golan Heights. Both Syria and Israel maintain important military posts on the mountain. Hermon's steep, rugged slopes are famous for their ski runs even though the ski areas are adjacent to several mine fields.

Mountains of Ararat (air-uh-rat)

Itinerary: Genesis 8:4-22

Traveler: Noah

Destination: mountains of Ararat

Topography: The mountains of Ararat were located in Armenia, also called the "land of Ararat" between the Black and Caspian Seas. The Tigris and Euphrates Rivers flowed from this range whose elevation ranged from 6,000 feet to 17,000 feet at Mount Ararat.

Transportation: ark

What to Take: The Lord told Noah to take his family, two of every animal, and food.

Arrival: prehistory

Reason for Visit: Many people began to populate the land. Their hearts were bent toward evil, and only one man, Noah, still walked with God. The Lord decided to destroy all the life on earth except Noah. He told him to build an ark and gave him precise instructions. When it was completed, Noah, his family, and two of every animal went inside. For 40 days and nights it rained until floodwaters covered even the mountains. Every living thing was destroyed, but the ark floated safely. After 150 days, the water receded, and the ark came to rest on the mountains of Ararat. When the earth was dry, Noah and his family left the ark to begin a new life.

Mountains of Ararat

Things to Do: Noah built an altar on the new earth and made sacrifices to God. Then God made a covenant with Noah, his sons, and their descendants. He promised never again to destroy life with a flood, and he sent a rainbow as a sign of his promise. Noah was 600 years old when the flood came and he was 950 years old when he died.

Then and Now: While the Bible only mentions the "mountains of Ararat," many believe that it was probably Great Ararat where the ark came to rest. Mount Ararat or Agri, located in eastern Turkey near the Iranian border, begins its ascent at an elevation of 8,880 feet and rises to two peaks: snow covered Great Ararat at 16,854 feet and Little Ararat at 12,840 feet.

Beroso, an astronomer and Babylonia historian, wrote in 275 B.C. of pilgrims who climbed Ararat to scrape away pitch on the side of the ark to make amulets. In 1269 Marco Polo wrote in his book "Il Milione,". . . and you should know that in that far off land of Armenia, Noah's ark still lies there on top of a high mountain with snows so persistent that nobody is able to climb it." Armenians say that in the turn of the century groups of villagers were guided up the Great Trail of Ararat to see the ark.

The search for Noah's ark is ongoing today with numerous reports of possible sightings. It is a challenging journey. The terrain is steep and the summit of Great Ararat is consumed by a glacier, under which many believe the ark might be resting.

In addition, access to the mountain is limited. It is an area of political unrest and since 1991 when Kurdish rebels kidnapped five archaeologists, the Turks closed Mount Ararat to outside visitors. Special permits are required and these are difficult to obtain.

Mount of Beatitudes (mount uhv bee-at-i-toodz)

Itinerary: Matthew 5

Traveler: Jesus

Destination: Mount of Beatitudes

Topography: The Mount of Beatitudes overlooked the Sea of Galilee just south of Capernaum. The mountain, also called Kuran Hattin or "Horns of Hattin," rose 1,135 feet above sea level to its summit which was capped with two cones or "horns."

Transportation: foot

What to Take: Jesus' disciples joined him on the mountainside.

Arrival: A.D. 30-31

Reason for Visit: Jesus climbed a mountain, later called the Mount of Beatitudes, and spent the night in prayer and meditation. The following morning, he called his disciples to him and chose twelve men to train as his apostles. They followed Jesus to a more level place where he delivered his longest recorded teaching called

Mount of Beatitudes

the "Sermon on the Mount" to a huge crowd. Jesus spoke of the "beatitudes"—short statements which began with the word *blessed* or *happy* which described the ideal character he desired in his followers.

"Blessed are the pure in heart, for they will see God," Jesus told them. He also taught about the importance of prayer, loving your enemies, giving to the needy and much more.

Things to Do: The word apostle means "one who is chosen and sent." The original twelve which Jesus chose included Peter, Andrew, James the son of Zebedee, John, Philip, Bartholomew, Thomas, Matthew, James the son of Alphaeus, Simon the Zealot, Thaddeus, and Judas Iscariot. Matthias replaced Judas when Judas committed suicide. Paul, also, was an important apostle.

Then and Now: Tradition more than evidence has long associated the "Sermon on the Mount" with Kuran Hattin. The actual spot on the mountain has been debated. Some think the famous sermon was delivered on the lower southern slope, while others believe it occurred on the platform between the two horned summits. The latter spot was considered a natural amphitheater largely due to the winds which blew off the Sea of Galilee and carried a speaker's voice up and down the mountain. The Church of the Beatitudes was built in 1937 directly on top of the mountain and is home to many monks. It commands a breathtaking view of the sea and the Jordan Valley and is, in fact, the only building on the mount. A portion of each of the beatitudes is written on each window of the cupola or domed roof.

Today, the Mount of Beatitudes is located halfway up Israel's Golan Heights. Huge buses come and go all day, carrying tourists up the mount and to the church. Nearby, a piece of the past has been preserved. A dirt road not far from the church is the original Roman road which was used as the major passageway between the Galilee valley and the Jordan valley. In late afternoons, young shepherds carry their staffs and lead their sheep down the dirt road from the higher pastures of the Golan Heights to the Galilee valley below.

<u>Mount of Olives</u> (mount uhv awl-ivz)

Itinerary: Acts 1:6-12

Traveler: Jesus

Destination: Mount of Olives

Topography: The Mount of Olives, also known as Mount Olivet, was a limestone ridge covered with olive groves and part of a range of hills east of Jerusalem. It was separated from the city by the Kidron Valley or Valley of Jehosophat. About a mile long and 2,600 feet above sea level, it was the highest hill in the area, even measuring about 250 feet higher than the temple mount.

Transportation: foot

What to Take: Jesus met his disciples there: Peter, John, James, Andrew, Philip, Thomas, Bartholomew, Matthew, James son of Alphaeus, Simon the Zealot and Judas, son of James

Arrival: A.D. 33

Reason for Visit: After Jesus was resurrected, he appeared to his disciples many times during the course of forty days. During these visits, he taught them more about the Kingdom of God. On the fortieth day, he met with them on the Mount of Olives. He said that very soon the Holy Spirit would come to them. Then, he rose into the sky and a cloud hid him from view. Two angels appeared beside the disciples. They told the men that someday Jesus would return in the same way he left. This is known today as the Second Coming. Jesus told his disciples that no one but God knows the time or the date of the coming.

Things to Do: It was from the Mount of Olives that Jesus began his Triumphal Entry into Jerusalem the Sunday before his crucifixion. In the Garden of Gethsemane, near the base of the mount, Jesus cried out to God just before he was arrested and crucified.

Then and Now: In New Testament times, the Mount of Olives was a wooded retreat used by many, including Jesus, as a place of reflection away from the heat and noise of the city's crowded streets. It was an easy walk, only about three-quarters of a mile from Jerusalem, and Jesus often taught his disciples here. People also came to the hill country to gather branches from olive, myrtle, and palm trees in order to make booths.

When the Romans laid siege to Jerusalem in A.D. 70, they named one of the mount's peaks, "the Lookout," because it towered over the city. Roman legions had a large camp here and used the site as a vantage point during the war. Much earlier in history, the Mount of Olives was used by David as a route of escape and refuge from Absalom.

Today, the Mount of Olives in central Israel holds great historical and spiritual significance largely because of its association with Jesus. The Chapel of Ascension at the very top marks the place where Jesus ascended into heaven. Inside is a stone bearing his worn footprint.

At the western base of the mount is the Church of All Nations, so named because of the many nations which participated in its construction. It was built in 1919 on the approximate site of the Garden of Gethsemane where Jesus wept on a rock, known today as the Rock of Agony.

Stretching from the top of the Mount of Olives to the Kidron Valley below is the vast Prophets Cemetery. Many devout Jews have chosen to be buried here. They believe that when the Messiah returns, they will be among the first to greet him. The tombs of Zechariah, James and Absalom, the rebellious son of King David, as well as many prophets and kings are also in the valley.

<u>Mount Sinai</u> (mount sye-nye)

Itinerary: Exodus 3:1-12

Traveler: Moses

Destination: Mount Sinai

Topography: Mount Sinai, also known as Mount Horeb, was part of a range of mountains in the Desert of Sinai in the southern portion of the Sinai Peninsula. Its red granite peak rose about 7,000 feet into the air.

Transportation: foot

What to Take: Moses carried his shepherd's staff.

Arrival: 1279 B.C.

Reason for Visit: Moses was tending sheep in the desert near Mount Sinai when the angel of the Lord appeared to him in a burning bush. God called to him from within the bush and Moses answered. God told Moses that when he delivered the Israelites out of Egypt, Moses would be their leader, his brother Aaron

would be the spokesman before Pharaoh and a simple shepherd's staff would be used by God to perform miracles. Though Moses was filled with many doubts, God reassured him and he obeyed.

Things to Do: In the third month of the Israelite's exodus from Egypt, they arrived at the base of Mount Sinai and camped for about a year. God descended to the top of the mountain many times to speak to Moses.

He descended upon it in fire to meet the Israelites below, and with his finger he etched the Ten Commandments on two stone tablets.

Then and Now: Since ancient times Mount Sinai was regarded as a sacred mountain for both Christians and Muslims. While there are several different sites which historians say could be the biblical mount, most agree that the likely place is Jebel Musa, which is Arabic for "Mountain of Moses." It is located in the Sinai Peninsula of northeastern Egypt between the Gulf of Suez and the Gulf of Aqaba. The peaks surrounding Jebel Musa are sometimes referred to as the "holy mountains."

In the sixth century, the Emperor Justinian I established the Monastery of Saint Catherine at the base of the mountain. It is built around what is thought to be the site of the burning bush from which God spoke to Moses. It is still a functioning monastery today, and Christians from around the world continue to make pilgrimages to this holy place. Inside, there are priceless art treasures including the second largest collection of illuminated manuscripts in the world. Only the Vatican has more. A small chapel inside is sometimes referred to as the Skull House because it is where the skulls of the monastery's deceased monks are kept.

Three thousand stone steps, carved by the monks, wind up the mountainside from the monastery to an amphitheater called the "Seven Elders of Israel." An additional 750 steps lead to the summit where the Chapel of the Holy Trinity was built in 1934. It is a breathtaking view. The return trip down the mountain leads past the Fountain of Moses, a small chapel of the Virgin and two arches, the Gate of St. Stephen and the Gate of the Law.

Nazareth (naz-uh-reth)

Itinerary: Matthew 2:19-23

Traveler: Joseph and Mary

Destination: Nazareth

Topography: Nazareth was a small town in the lower region of Galilee. It sat in a valley of limestone hills with Mount Carmel and the Mediterranean to the west, Mount Tabor to the east and snowy Mount Hermon to the north. The Plain of Esdraelon stretched to the south. Nazareth was at the crossroads of many great caravan routes, including one road which brought travelers from Egypt to the interior of Asia. Due to their location, Nazarenes were in contact with people from all over the world. News reached them very quickly.

Transportation: possibly by donkey

What to Take: Joseph and Mary took their son, Jesus.

Arrival: about 4 B.C.

Reason for Visit: After Jesus was born in Bethlehem, Herod realized that what was prophesized had come true. He worried that this child called "the king of the Jews" would someday take his

throne. The angel of the Lord appeared to Joseph in a dream and told him to take Mary and Jesus and escape to Egypt. Meanwhile, in an attempt to kill Jesus, Herod ordered that all children two years old and younger in the vicinity of Bethlehem be killed.

After Herod died, Joseph was again instructed by an angel to return to Israel. Since Herod's son was reigning in the land of Judea, Joseph, Mary and Jesus returned to Nazareth in Galilee.

Things to Do: Jesus spent the first twenty years of his life in this small community, surrounded by hills. He was trained by his father, Joseph, as a carpenter and spent much time studying in the local synagogues.

Then and Now: Archaeological excavations conducted in 1955 at the site of ancient Nazareth revealed that the town was primarily an agricultural community. Grain storage bins were found as well as oil mills, mill stones and cisterns. The soft, chalky land of the valley made it easy to tunnel below and build underground rooms connected with the caves above. The remains of the ancient town are located near the Muslim village of en-Natzirah in lower Galilee and not far from modern Nazareth.

Today, Nazareth is spread over several hills and valleys. The Basilica of the Annunciation was built on the grotto or cave where Mary lived. The Roman Catholic Church is considered one of the most important sites in the Christian world and was just completed in 1966. The walls are covered with mosaics of Mary and Jesus created by artists from Japan and around the world.

Not far away is the Church of Mary's Well, a Greek Orthodox church which marks the approximate location of the well from which Mary drew water. Since Nazareth is mostly Arab today, it does not have a large Christian population. Many of the churches in the area are modest in size.

The Negev (neg-ev)

Itinerary: Numbers 13:1-33; Numbers 14

Traveler: Twelve spies

Destination: The Negev

Topography: The Negev was a desert region south of Judea which covered an area of about 5,000 square miles. It was triangular in shape with its base just above Beersheba and its apex at Elath. There were four distinct regions: a coastal plain in the northwest, a plateau in the center, mountains in the south central and a valley in the east. Oases were scattered between long stretches of barren wasteland.

Transportation: foot

What to Take: water and food to last through their journey in the desert

Arrival: 1273 B.C.

Reason for Visit: After the Israelites left the desert of Sinai and neared the Promised Land, Moses sent 12 leaders to spy out the land of Canaan. They were to go through the Negev and into the hill country and report their findings to him. After 40 days they returned. The land was fertile, they said, but the people were large like giants and the cities were walled.

The Israelites were discouraged and wouldn't listen to Moses. When they tried to enter Canaan without him, against God's will, they were badly beaten. Because of their continual disobedience, God allowed them to wander in the desert for an additional 40 years.

Things to Do: The Israelites were angry. They talked of stoning Moses, choosing a new leader and returning to Egypt. Moses pleaded to God to forgive them, and the Lord did as he asked. However, he promised that no one who had seen his glory, witnessed his miracles and still disobeyed him ten times would enter the Promised Land.

Then and Now: In the vast region of the Negev, less than ten inches of rain fell per year and much of the land was dry and sparse with little vegetation. At the few oases, like Ein Gedi and Jericho, shepherds and camel caravans refreshed their animals.

Nabatean nomads who roamed the Negev not only survived, but prospered in the desert wilderness. They were famous water conservationists who harnessed the water of the flash flood season by using cisterns, building reservoirs and constructing dams. They grew quite wealthy in the spice trade by leading the caravans carrying spices from Arabia and Somalia, north through the desert. When the Negev was incorporated into the Roman empire, the

Nabateans raised the thoroughbred horses which were raced in the Roman coliseums.

The Bedouins, also desert dwellers, were a common sight in the Negev. They moved frequently with their sheep, goats, donkeys and camels in tow, following the water sources and living off the land. Their black tents, made of woven goat's hair were resistant to the rain, wind and sun.

Today, the Bedouins can still be found in the Negev, often settled near towns like Beer Sheva. Here, they bring their handiwork such as woven rugs, cushions, camel saddles and Arab headdresses to sell on market day. Buyers and sellers conduct their business in silence, using long stares and occasional blinks and smiles to negotiate a price and wrap up a sale.

Nile River (nye-uhl riv-ur)

Itinerary: Exodus 1:12–2:10

Traveler: baby Moses

Destination: Nile River

Topography: The Nile was the longest river in the world. It flowed northward from east central Africa through Uganda, Sudan, Egypt and to the Great Sea for about 4,200 miles. It was the principal river of Africa and Egypt and was so essential to their existence that Egypt was even called "The gift of the Nile."

Transportation: a papyrus basket

What to Take: Moses was wrapped in Hebrew swaddling clothes.

Arrival: 1350 B.C.

Reason for Visit:
Moses was born in Egypt to Hebrew slaves. At that time, the Pharaoh ordered that all male Hebrew babies were to be killed. His mother hid him for three months and then put him in a papyrus basket in the Nile River.

Pharaoh's daughter found the basket and adopted Moses, but God allowed Moses' own mother to care for him when he was young.

Things to Do: Moses' mother hoped that someone, probably an Egyptian, would find her baby and care for it. She had no other choice if she wanted her son to live. She found papyrus reeds from the river to make the basket and tar to waterproof it.

Then and Now: It was along the banks of the ancient Nile that some of the earliest forms of civilization emerged. Its waters gave life to the great Sahara Desert in Northern Africa and the "Red Land" or desert of Egypt which covered more than 90 percent of the country. Most Egyptians lived on the riverbanks called the "Black Land" or beside the canals which extended from it.

Each year, Egyptians anxiously awaited the flooding of the Nile. To measure the river's rise and fall, they invented a unit of measurement called a nilometer. This instrument, usually a stone with horizontal lines, helped them to predict whether to expect a high Nile year and flooding or a low Nile year and drought. Flooding in the Nile Delta region in lower Egypt brought rich sediment over the banks which created a top soil ideal for crops. The delta region has long been regarded as one of the most fertile areas in the world.

Along the banks and in the irrigated valleys, Egyptians planted

Nile River

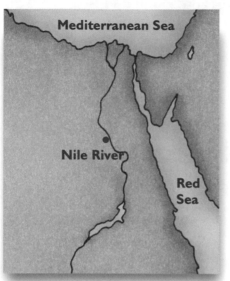

Mediterranean Sea

Nile River

Red Sea

wheat and barley and grew vegetables, fruit and flax. They grazed sheep, goats and cattle, particularly in the land of Goshen in the eastern Delta. Papyrus plants from the river were used to make the first paper known as papyrus. Since the Nile flowed north but the winds blew southerly, sailors could travel in either direction fairly easily between the cataracts or rapids.

Today, the Nile is still regarded as the source of life for both Africa and Egypt. It can be breathtakingly beautiful and many visitors cruise the river in feluccas or Nile river boats. In many places, it appears tame and friendly. Other parts remain mostly unnavigable and are wild, swarming with crocodiles and snakes.

Nineveh (nin-uh-vuh)

Itinerary: Jonah 1–3

Traveler: Jonah the prophet

Destination: Nineveh

Topography: The city of Nineveh was about 500 miles northeast of Israel in the land of Assyria. It stretched for 30 miles or more along the eastern bank of the Tigris River and about 10 miles back toward the eastern hills.

Transportation: foot

What to Take: Jonah carried a message from God for the people of Nineveh.

Arrival: 760-750 B.C.

Reason for Visit: The first time God told Jonah to go to Nineveh and preach against its wickedness, Jonah ran away. He boarded a ship to Tarshish and was swallowed by a great fish. After God delivered him and forgave him for his disobedience, God told Jonah once again to go to Nineveh. This time, Jonah obeyed. He entered the city and proclaimed, "Forty more days and Nineveh will be overturned."

When the king heard the news, he knew the prophetic message was from God. He took off his royal robes, covered himself with sackcloth and sat in the dust. He ordered his kingdom to fast and repent. When God saw that the people of Nineveh had turned from their evil ways, he had compassion and did not destroy them.

Nineveh

Things to Do: Jonah was not happy when God forgave Nineveh. He didn't think Gentiles should share in the message of God, which was why he ran away in the first place. He wanted the city destroyed because of its wickedness. God had to teach Jonah about compassion and mercy.

Then and Now: Like Babylon, Nineveh was founded by Nimrod, a great-grandson of Noah. It had massive defensive walls, broad, paved streets for three lanes of chariots, wide city squares, and public stores. There was a military garrison with stables, a parade ground, and an 80 room mansion called the "Palace Without a Rival."

Nineveh first served as an important religious center. Its political importance rose when it became the capital of the Assyrian Empire. Its strategic position on the highway between the Great Sea and the Indian Ocean contributed to its wealth. Gold and perfume arrived from Arabia and the Chaldean Sea. Linen, glasswork, carved enamels, tin and silver came from Egypt, and furs and iron from Asia Minor and Armenia. Nineveh, cruel and warlike, was a rival of the more cultured Babylon. For a short time, Babylon was brought into the Assyrian Empire, but the conquest didn't last long. In 612 B.C., Babylon helped contribute to the destruction of Nineveh.

Today, ruins of the ancient city are in northern Iraq. Excavations uncovered the palace of King Sennacherib. The Iraq Department of Antiquities roofed the walls of the throne room to form the Sennacherib Palace Site Museum. It is one of only two preserved Assyrian palaces in the world which visitors can tour. Also found was the huge library of King Ashurbanipal, the grandson of Sennacherib. About 10,000 cuneiform tablets survived from his collection of more than 20,000.

Patmos (pat-muhss)

Itinerary: Revelation 1:9

Traveler: John the Apostle

Destination: Patmos

Topography: Patmos, a rocky, volcanic island in the Aegean sea measuring ten miles long and six miles wide at its broadest point. Located about 35 miles offshore from the seacoast of Asia Minor, it was often used by Romans as a prison island or labor camp.

Transportation: grain ship or cargo vessel

What to Take: papyrus paper, ink, and split-reed pen

Arrival: about A.D. 95

Reason for Visit: John was sentenced to death for prophesying the return of Jesus. Prophecy of any sort was a crime against the Roman Empire. However, after he was tortured and did not die, the Roman Emperor Domitian sent

Patmos

John, who was 100 years old, to the island of Patmos to serve out the rest of his life. After about 18 months, with the fall of the Roman Empire near, John was freed by the new emperor, Nerva. He died about two years later at the age of 104. He was the last surviving Apostle.

Things to Do: John's life on Patmos probably consisted of hard labor. While exiled, God sent John remarkable visions. He wrote of these in a letter to seven churches called the Book of Revelation, the last book of the Bible.

Then and Now: Patmos was a barren island and nearly deserted during the Middle Ages. It was under Turkish rule until 1912 when it passed into the hands of Italy. In 1947 it was ceded to Greece.

Today, known as the "Jerusalem of the Aegean," Patmos has a population of slightly more than 2,000 and is a popular vacation spot. Part of the Northern Dodecanese Islands, between Leros and Ikaria, it is just west of present day Turkey. This lush island has many volcanic hills, rising as high as 800 feet. Its rugged coastline is filled with coves and many sandy beaches.

Near the harbor of Skala, the island's chief city, is the original cave or grotto in which John lived during his exile here. It is called the Cave of Revelation. In the hilltop city of Chora, with its twisting streets and white cube houses, rests the monastery of St. John. Its massive stone walls with battlements protected a main church and five chapels. In one chapel, frescos or paintings dating from A.D. 1210 to 1220 have been preserved. Today, the monastery also houses a museum which contains treasures from the Byzantine and post-Byzantine era. The library contains parchment documents, patriarchal seals, illuminated manuscripts and rare, old books. The monastery, by far the island's most important landmark, was built in the 11th century to honor the apostle known as "the disciple whom Jesus loved."

Philippi <u></u>(fil-i-pye)

Itinerary: Acts: 16:16-40

Traveler: Silas, a Christian leader

Destination: Philippi

Topography: The city of Philippi was once called Crenides, "the fountain." It was the capital of the province of Macedonia and was located near the head of the Aegean Sea, about eight miles from the port of Kavalla. The "Via Egnatia" or "Egnatian Way" was an important highway whose route through Greece passed through Philippi.

Transportation: cargo ship

What to Take: Silas accompanied Paul the apostle during his

second missionary journey.

Arrival: A.D. 50

Reason for Visit: When Silas and Paul were in Philippi, they met a slave girl possessed by a spirit which could tell the future. "In the name of Jesus Christ, I command you to come out of her!" Paul said. Instantly, the spirit left. When the owners realized the slave could no longer make money for them by telling fortunes, they dragged Silas and Paul to the authorities and accused them of breaking Roman law. The two missionaries were beaten and thrown into prison where their feet were placed in the stocks. At midnight, while they were praying and singing hymns, there was a violent earthquake. The prison doors flew open, and the prisoners' chains came loose.

Things to Do: Silas and Paul didn't escape. Instead, they witnessed to the jailor, and he and his whole family were saved. When the authorities tried to free them, Paul reminded them that their rights as Roman citizens had been violated when they were whipped and denied a fair trial. They wouldn't leave until they were personally escorted from the jail. Paul's letter to the Philippians, sent later, encouraged the church to be strong in the face of adversity.

Philippi

Then and Now: Philip II, the father of Alexander the Great, conquered this area in about 356 B.C. and renamed the town after himself. He liked the location of the city as well as the gold mines nearby. The city is best known for the famous Battle of Philippi which took place on the surrounding plain in 44 B.C.

After the assassination of Julius Caesar, Brutus and Cassius seized Macedonia and Syria and were in charge of all of the Roman Empire east of the Adriatic Sea. On the plains outside of Philippi, they were met by the combined forces of Mark Antony and Octavian, who later became Emperor Augustus. Cassius was defeated first, then Brutus, and both committed suicide.

Philippi's ruins near Kavala, Greece are considered one of the most important archaeological sites of eastern Macedonia. Excavations which began in 1914 uncovered an acropolis and its large medieval towers, an agora, several churches, and a public restroom with fifty marble toilets almost completely intact. An ancient theater was found and later restored and is used today for the performance of ancient dramas. It is believed that the prison where Paul and Silas were kept was once used as a Roman water cistern.

Pisidian Antioch (pi-sid-ee-uhn an-tee-ahk)

Itinerary: Acts 13:14-43

Traveler: Paul the apostle

Destination: Pisidian Antioch

Topography: Pisidian Antioch or "Antioch toward Pisidia" was located in Phrygia near Pisidia in southern Asia Minor. It was built on a plateau in the Taurus Mountains, 3,600 feet above sea level, overlooking the River Anthius. It was so named to distinguish it from other Antiochs, like the one in Syria.

Transportation: foot

What to Take: Barnabas accompanied Paul.

Arrival: A.D. 47

Reason for Visit: Paul and Barnabas traveled to Pisidian Antioch during Paul's first missionary journey. On the Sabbath, Paul taught about God's covenant with Israel, Jesus' resurrection, and how the gospel fulfilled the covenant. Paul and Barnabas were invited back the next week and the whole city was waiting to hear them. The Jews became jealous of the crowds, and spoke badly of the apostles. The Gentiles accepted the message and it spread in the region.

Paul and Barnabas were forced to leave the city, but they

were happy that the Gentiles believed God's Word.

Things to Do: The journey from Perga to Pisidian Antioch was 100 miles north on a dangerous mountain pass filled with hiding bandits. Before Paul and Barnabas ever started out, Paul became ill. They also received the disappointing news that their helper, John Mark, decided to return home to Jerusalem.

Then and Now: Pisidian Antioch was one of 16 Antiochs founded by Seleucus Nicator in honor of his father Antiochus. It was established in about 300 B.C. as a military outpost. Nearly 275 years later, it became a Roman colony and capital of the province of southern Galatia. It continued its military role and served as a Roman garrison in charge of subduing the wild tribes in the surrounding countryside.

Excavations of this city revealed important historical finds such as a marble portrait head of Emperor Augustus and 260 fragments of his autobiography. It was called "Res Gestae Divi Augusti" or "Statement of Achievements by the Divine Augustus." This copy was inscribed in stone in an important place in the city, probably a temple, to honor the emperor. Part of it said, "I drove into exile the murderers of my father (Julius Caesar), avenging their crime through tribunals established by law . . ." The original bronze inscription which once stood in front of the mausoleum of the Emperor Augustus in Rome has been lost.

Pisidian Antioch was believed destroyed by successive earthquakes. Portions of its marble streets are in the ruins of the ancient city near modern Yalvac in Turkey. Scattered throughout the area are the remains of aqueducts, a theater, public baths, a temple to Augustus and St. Paul's Basilica.

Ptolemais (tahl-uh-may-uhss)

Itinerary: Acts 21:7

Traveler: Paul the Apostle

Destination: Ptolemais

Topography: Ptolemais, originally called Accho, was a port city in Galilee located on the Great Sea between Tyre to the north and Caesarea to the south. It was one of Palestine's few good harbors and was on the Via Maris trade route. Ptolemais was often used as a port of entry for invading armies. Fortress walls and a moat surrounded the inner city.

Transportation: cargo ship

What to Take: Paul carried gifts sent from churches in Asia and Greece to give to needy Christians in Jerusalem.

Arrival: between A.D. 53-57

Reason for Visit: On Paul's third missionary journey he departed from Antioch. His final destination was Jerusalem, but he traveled through Asia, Macedonia and Greece to encourage the disciples and spread words of hope. On this journey, Paul witnessed great miracles and great hardship. Though the Holy Spirit forewarned him of the suffering he would endure when he reached Jerusalem, Paul pressed on. On the way from Tyre to

Caesarea, Paul landed in Ptolemais. He visited with his Christian friends for a day and then continued on his journey to Jerusalem.

Things to Do: Ptolemais was a bustling city filled with the sights and sounds of merchant ships loading and unloading their cargo, local fishing craft, foreign travelers talking of their journeys, and busy marketplaces.

Then and Now: The port of Ptolemais was a popular military target to those nations who wanted to conquer Israel. The city was heavily fortified, and yet it fell many times into the hands of the Greeks, Romans, Turks and Crusaders.

By the nineteenth century the once famous port had filled with silt, and the city went into decline. In 1918 it was captured from the Turks by the British army and used during World War II as a prison fortress. Members of the Jewish Resistance were imprisoned in the citadel. Then, on May 17, 1948, Israel won control of the city.

Today, Acre or Akko, as it is called, sits on the edge of the Mediterranean Sea along the Northern coast of Israel. Its fortress walls, rebuilt many times, still stand. In fact, it is only one of two cities in all of Israel whose ancient walls are completely intact. The other is the Old City in Jerusalem.

Akko is frequently visited by tourists who enjoy the charm of its winding streets and its traditional bazaars or open-air markets. Its rich history can be seen in the remains of the Roman aqueducts, the Turkish guardhouses and Turkish baths. The Great Mosque of al-Jazzar, the largest of many mosques in the city, is the major center of Islam in the Galilee region. Its columns and marble were taken from the ruins of the ancient cities of Caesarea, Ashkelon and Tyre.

Recent archeological digs have also uncovered the remains of an underground crusader city and an ancient two-mile tunnel which runs to the sea.

Red Sea (red see)

Itinerary: Exodus 14:5-28

Traveler: The pharaoh of Egypt

Destination: Red Sea

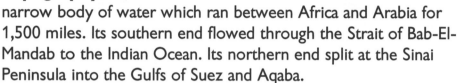

Topography: The Red Sea was a narrow body of water which ran between Africa and Arabia for 1,500 miles. Its southern end flowed through the Strait of Bab-El-Mandab to the Indian Ocean. Its northern end split at the Sinai Peninsula into the Gulfs of Suez and Aqaba.

Transportation: the pharaoh's chariot

What to Take: The Egyptian army, including 600 war chariots.

Arrival: 1275 B.C.

Reason for Visit: Moses led the Israelites out of Egypt toward the Red Sea. When the pharaoh realized they had left, he regretted his decision to let them go. He gathered his army and overtook the Israelites as they camped by the sea. "Do not be afraid," Moses told his people. "Stand firm and you will see the deliverance the Lord will bring you today." The angel of the Lord and the pillar of cloud which traveled in front of the Israelites moved behind, separating them from the Egyptians. Moses stretched his hand over the water, and the Lord blew the sea back with a strong east wind. The Israelites passed though the sea on dry land. When the Egyptians followed, their chariot wheels jammed. Again, Moses stretched his hand over the sea. At daybreak, the water flowed back, consuming the Egyptians, their horses and chariots.

Things to Do: The Egyptians had watch-posts throughout the Sinai Peninsula and messages were flashed from tower to tower by using reflected light. Some think this was how the pharaoh knew where the Israelites were. Many scholars believe Ramses II was the pharaoh who let the Israelites go.

Then and Now: The site of the Red Sea crossing is debated. Some think it was the Gulf of Suez, a northern arm of the sea. Others believe that since the translation of the Red Sea in Hebrew is "Reed Sea," it was probably a lake or swamp north of the gulf where reeds grow in abundance. Perhaps both are right. At the time of the Exodus, the Gulf of Suez extended at least 50 miles further north than it does today.

The Red Sea was an important trade route in antiquity. Solomon's "ships of Tarshish" navigated the Gulf of Aqaba and sailed to Arabia in search of gold, silver, and spices. Egyptian sailors loaded their ships with copper, cooking pots and clothing and traded them in the Indies for elephants, ebony and gems. When the Suez Canal was completed in 1869 connecting the Red Sea to the Mediterranean, the waterway became one of the chief shipping routes between Europe, East Asia and Australia.

The Red Sea is the only enclosed coral sea in the world. Today, The Coral World Underwater Observatory near the Port of Elat on the Gulf of Aqaba permits a view of the Red Sea's breathtaking coral reef and the thousands of exotic fish and marine life which live there.

Rome (rohm)

Itinerary: Acts 28:11-30

Traveler: Paul the apostle

Destination: Rome

Topography: Rome, the "Eternal City," was on the Tiber River in Central Italy, about ten miles from the western coast and the Tyrrhenian Sea. It was built amidst the Seven Hills called the Capitoline, Quirinal, Viminal, Esquiline, Caelian, Aventine, and Palatine.

Transportation: Egyptian grain ship

What to Take: Paul was escorted by Julius the centurion, Luke and Aristarchus.

Arrival: A.D. 60

Reason for Visit: The end of Paul's third missionary journey brought him to Rome where he hoped to appeal to Caesar against the charges brought against him by Jews in Jerusalem. Though he was under house arrest and guarded by a soldier, he was afforded the luxury of living in his own

rented house and was allowed to receive visitors. It is believed he was released after two years and may have begun a fourth missionary journey, possibly venturing as far as Spain. Once again, Paul was taken prisoner in Rome, but this time he was kept in close confinement until his execution. He was beheaded in late 66 or early 67 under the direction of Emperor Nero.

Things to Do: Peter, too, was martyred around the same time in Rome. It is said he was crucified upside down because he did not feel worthy to die in the same manner as his Lord.

Then and Now: Tradition says two brothers, Romulus and Remus, were left to drown at the edge of the flooded Tiber River and found by a she-wolf who raised them. As men, they returned to the same spot on the Tiber where they founded Rome in 753 B.C. Rome was a center of higher learning, art, music and philosophy and it soon grew to over one million people. As capital of The Roman Empire, it was led by brilliant commanders such as Julius Caesar, Mark Antony and Octavian.

Rome's extensive history is reflected in its ruins. The Colosseum with its removable canvas roof was the city's grandest amphitheater. It was built over a drained artificial lake on the grounds of Nero's Golden House. Large crowds cheered the bloody duels of gladiators, slaves and wild animals. A cross at the edge of the arena pays tribute to the many Christians who died there.

The Circus Maximus, the largest structure ever built for entertainment held over 350,000 people and was flooded with millions of gallons of water in order to stage mock sea battles.

It is believed that either Peter's death or burial took place on Vatican Hill where the Basilica St. Peter was built. A gate in the historic Aurelian Wall which still encloses central Rome was renamed Porta San Paolo, in honor of the apostle Paul who passed through it on the way to his execution.

Samaria (suh-mair-ee-uh)

Itinerary: 2 Kings 10:17-28

Traveler: Jehu, tenth king of Israel

Destination: Samaria

Topography: The city of Samaria, "watch-tower," was several miles northwest of Shechem in the mountains of Israel, east of the Great Sea. It was built on top of the high "hill of Shomeron" which had steep slopes and a flat summit and overlooked Jerusalem to its north.

Transportation: chariot

What to Take: Jehonadab, son of Recab, went with Jehu.

Arrival: 841 B.C.

Reason for Visit: When Jehu was a commander in the army, he was anointed by a prophet to succeed Israel's King Jehoram, son of the wicked Ahab. The prophet told Jehu that the Lord wanted him to destroy the whole house of Ahab. Jehu accepted his calling and killed King Jehoram, King Ahaziah of Judah, Jezebel, seventy

young princes and everyone in Jezreel who remained in the house of Ahab.

Then, the new king went to Samaria. He gathered all of the followers of the pagan god Baal in the temple built by Ahab and Jezebel. He ordered his guards to kill them and destroy the sacred stone of Baal. The temple was torn down and used as a latrine.

Things to Do: Ahab and Jezebel led Israel in the worship of pagan gods like Baal. Although King Jehu destroyed Baal worship in Israel, he did not stop the Israelites from worshiping the golden calves at Bethel and Dan.

Then and Now: King Omri of Israel bought the "hill of Shomeron" for two talents of silver. He worked on the construction of Samaria for the last six years of his reign and established it as the capital of the Kingdom of Israel in the north. It was the only major city founded by the ancient Hebrews. Ahab, Omri's son, later became king and also ruled Israel from Samaria. He built a splendid palace made of ivory and a temple dedicated to the worship of Baal. He was later buried here as were other Israelite kings who had lived in the city.

Samaria was frequently attacked and sometimes conquered and rebuilt. At one point it was given to Herod the Great by the emperor Augustus. Herod rebuilt it and renamed it Sebaste, a Greek form of Augustus, in honor of the emperor. The apostle Philip centered his ministry in the region of Samaria, making it one of the first places outside of Jerusalem where the message of Jesus was delivered.

Today, Samaria is a small village called Sebustieh. The many ruins of the ancient town are scattered over the hill, some having rolled down the slopes. The shafts of about 100 ornate Corinthian columns are still standing, and more than 200 ivory plaques were discovered in a storeroom near the remains of a palace. It is believed the ivory may have been used to make the furniture in Ahab's ivory home. A large pool or reservoir was also discovered in the palace remains. Scholars think it was probably the one used to wash Ahab's bloodstained chariot as noted in 1 Kings 22:38.

Sea of Galilee (see uhv gal-i-lee)

Itinerary: Luke 8:22-25

Traveler: Jesus

Destination: Sea of Galilee

Topography: The Sea of Galilee, also called the Sea of Kinnereth or Lake Tiberias, was referred to as "the lute" because of its pear shape. It was actually a freshwater lake east of Galilee and 60 miles north of Jerusalem. It was in a volcanic basin about 685 feet below sea level and was surrounded by mountains. The Jordan River poured into it, providing a constant source of fresh water.

Transportation: fishing boat

What to Take: Jesus' disciples went with him.

Arrival: A.D. 30

Reason for Visit: Jesus told his disciples one day that he wanted to go to the other side of the Sea of Galilee. As they sailed, Jesus fell asleep and a sudden storm came upon them, filling the boat with water. The disciples, fearing they would drown, awakened the Lord. Jesus arose and asked them, "Where is your faith?" He spoke to the wind and the water, and at once the storm subsided and the sea was calm again.

The disciples were amazed that even the wind and the water obeyed him.

Things to Do: Jesus found his first disciples on the shores of the Sea of Galilee. Simon, called Peter; his brother Andrew; James, son of Zebedee, and his brother John were all fishermen. Jesus called them to be with him, and they became fishers of men.

Then and Now: Nine bustling cities, each with a population of 15,000 or more, once populated the banks of the biblical lake. Fish was an important part of the diet, even more so than meat, and this lake was the principal source. It was about 13 miles long, 8 miles wide and up to 150 feet deep in parts. It supplied enough fish to feed the entire region and beyond. Capernaum and other towns nearby enjoyed a prosperous fishing industry by supplying the entire Roman Empire with large quantities of salted, dried fish.

Fisherman used casting nets and dragnets and occasionally, hooks and anchors. Legend says that when Jesus told Peter to take a coin from the mouth of a fish to pay a tax, the fish was a "Tiliapia galilea" upon which Peter left his fingerprints. The species is identified today by markings which closely resemble fingerprints.

The Sea of Galilee is as unpredictable today as it was in ancient times. Though it is often calm in the mornings, late afternoons can bring sudden, violent storms with waves as high as 20 feet. Of its nine ancient towns, only Tiberias exists today. In 1987 excavations finally began on the lost city of Bethsaida, once located on its shores.

A Galilean fishing boat, over 2,000 years old, was discovered in 1985, partially imbedded in the clay sea bottom which had receded during a drought. It is on display in the local Beit Allon Museum which contains many archaeological finds from the area.

Another drought several years later made the level of the lake drop dramatically again, revealing a 20,000-year-old encampment. Hundreds of grains, the oldest ever discovered at an archaeological site, were found.

Shechem (shek-uhm)

Itinerary: Joshua 24:1-28

Traveler: Joshua

Destination: Shechem

Topography: The city of
Shechem was about 35 miles
north of Jerusalem and 23
miles east of the Great Sea in
north-central Palestine. It was
located in the beautiful valley
between Mount Gerazim, "the Mount
of Blessing," and Mount Ebal, "the Mount of
Cursing." It was a major stop along the King's Highway, the inland
international trade route which linked Egypt and Mesopotamia.

Transportation: foot

What to Take: The Israelites

Arrival: 1200 B.C.

Reason for Visit: Joshua was very old when he gathered the
tribes of Israel in Shechem for a final meeting before his death. He
reminded them of how God had taken care of them on their
journey to the Promised Land. Then he asked them to choose again
whom they would worship—God or pagan idols. The Israelites

answered, "We will serve the Lord our God and obey him!" On that day, Joshua renewed the covenant between Israel and God. He drew up decrees and laws for the people and recorded them in the Book of the Law of God. Then he placed a large stone under an oak tree as a witness to the covenant the Israelites had renewed with God on that day. This was the second time that Joshua made a covenant between Israel and God in the area of Shechem.

Things to Do: The valley between Mount Gerazim, 2,849 feet, and Mount Ebal, 3,077 feet, was only about 500 yards long. It formed a natural amphitheater so Joshua could be easily heard. He died not long after at the age of 110.

Then and Now: Shechem was an important city in biblical history. Abraham left Haran and traveled to Shechem where God appeared to him and promised the land to his descendants. He built an altar here which for many centuries stood as an historical landmark.

Jacob bought property in this ancient town and dug a well. When Israel entered the Promised Land, the bones of his son Joseph were taken from Egypt to Shechem and buried on his father's property.

Shechem was not destroyed when the Promised Land was taken by the Israelites. Instead, it served as the first religious and political center of the Israelite tribes.

It was one of Israel's six cities of refuge where a person who accidentally killed another could be safe until he could have a fair trial. The city declined in importance only when Jerusalem was selected as the capital.

Today, the site of the biblical city is known as Tell Balatah, just east of Nablus on the West Bank. Jacob's well has survived and is one of the oldest continuously used artifacts on earth. It is about seven and a half feet in diameter and about 100 feet deep. The water which once refreshed Jesus is still good and quenches the thirst of visitors today. It belongs to the Greek Orthodox Church which has built a large, unfinished church over the site. The tomb of Joseph has also remained intact.

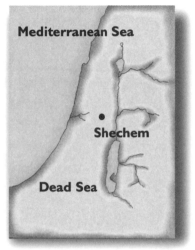

Sidon (sye-don)

Itinerary: Acts 27:1-3

Traveler: Luke, "beloved physician"

Destination: Sidon

Topography: Sidon, "fishery," was a city and seaport on the Great Sea, about 25 miles north of Tyre in the region of Phoenicia. The town was on a rocky outcropping overlooking the sea. Several offshore islands were connected to the mainland by piers and the area between formed its port. It was a prosperous trade and fishing center.

Transportation: cargo ship

What to Take: Luke and Aristarchus accompanied Paul who was guarded by Julius, a Roman centurion.

Arrival: about A.D. 59

Reason for Visit: At the end of Paul's third missionary journey, he was persecuted by Jews in Jerusalem and placed under house arrest. He began a long and difficult journey to Rome where he desired that his case be heard by Caesar. On the way, he spent two years imprisoned in Caesarea. When he was finally allowed to set sail for Rome, his close friend Luke accompanied him. The boat docked in Sidon and Julius allowed Paul to visit with friends. Luke stayed with Paul until the end of his first imprisonment in Rome.

Things to Do: The Gospel of Luke and Acts of the Apostles were both written by Luke. He was a well-educated Gentile doctor, an evangelist and Paul's frequent traveling companion. His writings, polished and descriptive, provided an orderly, historically accurate account of the life and works of Jesus and some of the apostles. It is possible that Luke was martyred in Greece.

Then and Now: Sidon was the chief city of Phoenicia and the mother city of Tyre. It was the first home of the Phoenicians on the coast of Palestine and was responsible for sending the first Phoenician ships out to sea, colonizing as far as Malta. Sidon grew into a huge naval power and trade center, importing copper from Cyprus, linen from Egypt, ivory from India, tin from Spain, horses from Anatolla and peacocks from Africa. The country exported timber from its forests and red and purple dye extracted from the shell of the murex snail. Sidonians were also expert craftsmen, highly skilled in the art of glass blowing and metal works. They left behind many ornate silver bowls, cups trimmed in gold and glassware.

Though the great city fell many times into the hands of Assyria, Babylon, Persia, Greece and Rome, it always rose again. Today, it is called Saida and is located south of Beirut in Lebanon. Excavations of the ancient city revealed a large cemetery and the skeleton of a woman who belonged to the royal family. She wore a crown with blue and green jewels, rings with precious stones and anklets. The shell of the Castle of St. Louis sits on top of the acropolis near Murex Hill. A thirteenth century Castle by the Sea, built by Crusaders as a fortress, still guards the mouth of the north harbor. Today, fishermen cast their lines into the sea from the castle walls.

Sodom and Gomorrah (sod-uhm and guh-mor-uh)

Itinerary: Genesis 19:1-29

Traveler: two angels

Destination: Sodom

Topography: Sodom and Gomorrah were two of the five "Cities of the Plain" which also included Admah, Zeboiim and Zoar. They were located somewhere around the area of the Salt Sea on the fertile Jordanian Plain.

Transportation: probably foot

What to Take: The two angels carried a message from the Lord for Lot and his family.

Arrival: 1975 B.C.

Reason for Visit: God decided to visit Sodom and Gomorrah when his people cried out to him about the wickedness of these cities. Abraham asked God if he would save any righteous people who lived there so the Lord sent two angels to Sodom who stayed at the home of Lot. When men from the town tried to break into Lot's house and hurt the angels, the men were struck blind. The angels led Lot, his wife and two daughters out of the city and told them not to look back. Once they were safely away in the town of Zoar, burning sulfur rained down from heaven and destroyed Sodom, Gomorrah, Admah, Zeboiim, and much of the Jordanian plain. When Lot's wife disobeyed and glanced back, she was turned into a pillar of salt.

Things to Do: While Sodom and Gomorrah were very prosperous cities, their people were very wicked. They sinned against God on a regular basis and practiced every kind of immoral and perverse act.

Then and Now: Sodom and Gomorrah were surrounded by the lush, watered land of the Jordanian Plain. It was here that Lot parted company with Abraham and chose this attractive country for his home, leaving his uncle the less fertile land of Canaan. After the cities were destroyed, the land became barren.

Though Sodom and Gomorrah are classified as "lost," it is widely believed that their remains lie beneath the Dead Sea. Whether it is the northern end or the southern end is still disputed.

The Dead Sea is really a lake and lies between Israel and Jordan. It is known to the Arabs as Bahr Lut which means the "Sea of Lot." With an elevation of 1,300 feet below sea level, it is the lowest point on earth. It is seven times as salty as the ocean, making it extremely buoyant. Its high concentration of other minerals such as calcium, potassium, magnesium and bromide make the water very therapeutic but bitter to taste and oily to touch. Signs are posted along many of the beaches in Hebrew, Aramaic, and English, warning the bathers not to drink the water and not to splash on other swimmers.

The Dead Sea is fed mainly by the Jordan River with no less than six million tons of water every day.

Though the lake has no outlet, its level is maintained by pure evaporation, sometimes so intense that a thick blue haze is formed over the surface of the lake. Chunks of pure salt, as large as automobiles, are formed after the water has evaporated. While the Dead Sea cannot sustain any life—fish dumped into the water from the Jordan River die almost immediately—an abundance of wildlife lives on its banks, feeding on the dead fish which wash ashore.

Syracuse (sihr-uh-kyooss)

Itinerary: Acts 27:27–28:1, 11-14

Traveler: Paul the apostle

Destination: Syracuse

Topography: Syracuse was a city on the southeast coast of the island of Sicily. The original town was built on Ortygia Island, just off the coast, but its city limits soon extended to the mainland where it was connected by a canal. It had two excellent harbors which contributed to the wealth of the city.

Transportation: Egyptian grain ship

What to Take: Luke accompanied Paul on this journey.

Arrival: A.D. 59

Reason for Visit: At the end of Paul's third missionary journey, he was allowed to sail to Rome in protective custody. Here, he could defend himself as a Roman citizen against the charges of the Jews. On his way there, his ship was wrecked in a bay off the coast of Malta. He was forced to spend three months on the island waiting until the passing of the winter storm season. He set sail again, traveling 100 miles to Syracuse where he stayed for three days before journeying on.

Things to Do: Since ancient sailors did not have compasses to guide them, they relied solely on the stars to navigate their course. Sailing in the winter months was considered unwise because frequent storms brought cloudy skies and strong, unpredictable winds. Paul's ship set sail at the advent of the storm season.

Then and Now: Syracuse was founded by colonists from the Greek city-state of Corinth in 734 B.C. It was once a magnificent Greek city which developed into a great power under the rule of tyrant Dionysius the Elder.

The famous Greek mathematician and engineer, Archimedes, was born in Syracuse. When the Romans laid siege to the city in 212 B.C., he was credited with its defense. He invented the cranes which pulled the Roman ships from the water and flung them against the

cliffs, and he also developed the catapult. Unfortunately, Syracuse fell to the Romans and Archimedes was killed at the hands of a Roman soldier.

Today, Syracuse is the capital of Syracuse Province in Sicily. Remains of the ancient city, which are mostly on Ortygia Island, include the largest Greek theater in Sicily. It is cut entirely out of rock, can hold 15,000 spectators and has been used to stage tragedies since the fifth century. It is still used today for performances by the Institute of Ancient Drama. A Roman amphitheater, also carved from rock, was erected in the second century. A corridor was unearthed beneath the arena with entrances which were used by the gladiators and wild animals.

In 1608, famed Italian painter Michelangelo Merisi, also known as Caravaggio, stayed in Syracuse for a time and painted some of his last canvases. "The Burial of Saint Lucy" and "The Raising of Lazarus" have remained in Sicily and are on display.

Tarshish (tar-shish)

Itinerary: Jonah 1:1–2:10

Traveler: Jonah the Prophet

Destination: Tarshish

Topography: Tarshish is often identified with the ancient Phoenician port of Tartessus which was located along the Atlantic coast of Spain between the two mouths of the river Guadalquivir.

Transportation: merchant ship

What to Take: Jonah carried the word of the Lord with him, even though he chose to ignore it for a time.

Arrival: 760-750 B.C.

Reason for Visit: The Lord spoke to the prophet Jonah and told him to go to Nineveh and preach against the wickedness there. Instead, Jonah ran away to Joppa and boarded a ship sailing to Tarshish. While Jonah was sleeping below the deck, a violent storm arose and tossed the ship to and fro. The sailors were afraid, and they cast lots to find out who was responsible for their calamity. When the lot fell on Jonah, they asked him, "What should we do to you, to make the sea calm down for us?"

Jonah replied, "Pick me up and throw me into the sea, and it shall become calm again." The sailors tried to row back, but they could not. They threw Jonah into the sea and the storm stopped. The sailors turned to God, prayed, and vowed to serve him.

Things to Do: When Jonah was tossed overboard, he was swallowed by a great fish. For three days and three nights, he sat in the fish's belly. Jonah felt as though he had been buried alive, but he gave thanks to God that he was not dead. The Lord commanded the fish to spit Jonah out onto dry land. For the second time, God told Jonah to go to Nineveh, and this time the prophet obeyed.

Then and Now: There is no conclusive evidence as to the whereabouts of the lost Tarshish. Many associated the city with India, probably because Solomon's fleet of trading ships called the "ships of Tarshish," sailed to India every three years. They were manned by the sailors of Tyre, known for their sailing expertise, and returned laden with treasures of gold, silver, ivory, apes and baboons. Some thought Tarshish was actually the ancient city of Carthage in North Africa.

Most, however, believe that the most likely place for its existence was in Spain. Ancient historians gave Spain many different names throughout history, one of them being Tartessos.

The city of like name was a Carthaginian colony in Spain and the most western port for Tyrian sailors, also known for their vast exploration of the seas. Tartessus was called the "Peru of Tyrian adventure" because it was wealthy with silver, copper and gold. It had a lucrative trade with Phoenicia, Carthage, Brittany and south-west Britain.

The city was believed destroyed in about 500 B.C. by the Carthaginians. Excavations were conducted in 1981 in an area below the modern city of Huelva. A clay crucible with traces of silver in it was found in addition to Bronze Age pottery.

Tarsus (tar-suhss)

Itinerary: Acts 9:26-30

Traveler: Saul of Tarsus

Destination: Tarsus

Topography: The city of Tarsus was in a prime location within the province of Cilicia. It stood on the fertile Cilician Plain along the Cydnus River, about ten miles inland from the Great Sea. It was close to the Cilician Gates, the pass through the Taurus mountains which was on the major trade route between Syria and Asia Minor.

Transportation: ship

What to Take: Saul nearly always carried the supplies he used as a tentmaker.

Arrival: about A.D. 37

Reason for Visit: After Saul's conversion to Christianity in Damascus, he fled the city, pursued by angry Jews who felt betrayed.

He traveled to Arabia and stayed there for three years, spending time with God. He hoped his long absence would give the Pharisees plenty of time to cool down. When he finally returned to Jerusalem, the disciples did not believe he was really converted.

181

Tarsus

Barnabas convinced them of Saul's sincerity and for a time, Saul moved about the city, preaching in the name of Jesus. When Grecian Jews tried to kill him, the disciples accompanied Saul to Caesarea where he was sent off to Tarsus.

Things to Do: Saul was born in the city of Tarsus about the same time that Jesus was born in Bethlehem. He spent the early part of his youth in this city of Jews and Greeks. He was learned in the Bible, Stoic philosophy, and the Greek language. Later, he moved to Jerusalem. He once said of the city of his youth, "I am a Jew, from Tarsus in Cilicia, a citizen of no ordinary city."

Then and Now: Tarsus was a fortified city and trade center as early as 2000 B.C. The Cydnus River, upon which it sat, provided an easy exit to the sea with a dock and a harbor. The Taurus mountains, with peaks as high as 11,000 feet above sea level, provided a trade route between the east and the west through the mountain pass, The Cilician Gates. It is believed that Paul took this same route through the pass during his second and third missionary journeys.

Tarsus was also a commercial center. Linen was woven from the flax which grew in the fertile plains, and cilicium was woven from goat's hair and used to make coverings which protected against the cold and the rain. After the Romans conquered Tarsus in the first century B.C., it became Cilicia's chief city and one of the most important in Asia Minor. It was a cosmopolitan center of learning—a university town, home to several well-known scholars including the Stoic philosopher Athenodorus.

Today, Tarsus is in southern Turkey between Adana and the port city of Mersin. Remnants of the ancient city include St. Paul's Well, and a well by the traditional site of Saul's birthplace. A plaque commemorating Paul's work was placed by the well in the city of Tarsus. The water is considered by many to be holy. The River Cydnus once brought Cleopatra to Tarsus to meet Mark Antony. A stone arch, once the sea gate which led to the walled city, is known today as Cleopatra's Gate or St. Paul's Gate.

Thessalonica (thess-uh-loh-nye-kuh)

Itinerary: Acts 17:1-10

Traveler: Paul the apostle

Destination: Thessalonica

Topography: Thessalonica was the capital city of the Roman province of Macedonia and was very wealthy. It was situated on two major trade routes at the head of the Thermaic Gulf. Its fairly sheltered harbor made it the chief port of Macedonia.

Transportation: foot

What to Take: Paul's friends and helpers Saul and Timothy went with him.

Arrival: A.D. 51

Reason for Visit: On Paul's second missionary journey, he traveled to Thessalonica. On the Sabbaths, he preached in the Jewish synagogue about Jesus. The Jews were jealous of the number of people who came to hear Paul, so they formed a mob and started a riot. The mob went to the house of Jason where the missionaries were staying, but when they discovered that they weren't there,

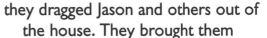

they dragged Jason and others out of the house. They brought them before city officials and made accusations against them. Jason and the others had to put up cash before they were freed. In the night, Paul, Silas and Timothy slipped away.

Things to Do: Paul attracted a number of wealthy followers in Thessalonica and the church grew quickly. Though he was forced to flee, he sent Timothy back to see how the church was doing. He wrote the church two letters, First and Second Thessalonians, in which he encouraged the believers to remain faithful.

Then and Now: Ancient Thessalonica was established in about 316 B.C. by Cassander, a Macedonian general. It was named after his wife, Thessalonica, the sister of Alexander the Great. The city was built on the site of the ancient town of Therme, which gave its name to the Thermaic Gulf. It became the second most important city of the Byzantine Empire, next to Constantinople. Its use of many coins meant that it was a prosperous city and its majestic architecture also spoke of wealth.

In 1492 20,000 Jews fled from Spain to Thessalonica. Skilled in working with wool, silk, and precious stones, they formed a group of craftsman and merchants who traded throughout Europe, bringing further wealth into the city. They were an interesting group of people who wore caftans and greatcoats trimmed in fur. By 1910, the Jewish community made up half of the population of the city. Thessalonica, which was under Turkish rule, was returned to Greece in 1912.

During World War I, it was headquarters to the allied armies in the East, and during World War II, it was occupied by the Germans who deported about 50,000 Jews.

Today, known as Thessaloniki or Salonika, it is one of the largest cities in Greece and is the main port and commercial center of Macedonia. Each year it hosts the International Trade Fair. It is also an important cultural center and is home to the Greek Film Festival, the Greek Light Song Festival and the internationally famous Theatre of Northern Greece.

<u>Tyre</u> (tire)

Itinerary: Matthew 15:21-28

Traveler: Jesus

Destination: Tyre

Topography: Tyre was a great trading port of ancient Phoenicia. It was located on a small, rocky island in the Great Sea about a half mile from shore and 25 miles south of Sidon. It offered one of the best harbors on the coast. The island fortress was virtually impregnable until Alexander the Great built a causeway from the mainland to the island in 332 B.C. and stormed the city.

Transportation: most likely by foot.

What to Take: Jesus always took the compassion and love of his Heavenly Father when he traveled and ministered to the people.

Arrival: A.D. 31

Reason for Visit: A Canaanite woman whose daughter was demon-possessed came to Jesus and asked for help. Through a parable, Jesus explained that Jews were given the first opportunity

to accept him as Messiah so they could spread the message of salvation to the rest of the world. When the woman continued to show great faith in him, her daughter was immediately healed.

Things to Do: The citizens of Tyre often traveled to Galilee to hear Jesus preach. During Paul's third missionary journey, he and Luke spent seven days visiting with the small Christian community while they waitied for their ship to be unloaded.

Then and Now: Though ancient Tyre was founded in about 2740 B.C. as a modest island city, it soon developed into the most important trading port in the Phoenician empire. Tyre's sailors shocked the world when they explored the Great Sea, sailing as far west as Spain and Britain and circumnavigating Africa in 600 B.C. King Hiram of Tyre supplied Solomon's Red Fleet with his sailors—the only ones thought skilled enough to navigate the treacherous Gulf of Aqabah in search of gold.

Tyre's merchants, known as "princes of the sea," traded in metals such as copper from Cyprus, tin from Cornwall and silver from Spain. They supplied King David with cedars, carpenters, masons, and bronzesmiths with which to build his palace.

In the eighteenth century, Tyre became famous for its beautiful purple dye which was used to color fabric. The dye was extracted a few drops at a time from the murex, a shellfish found in the local waters. It was an expensive process and only the very wealthy, such as kings and queens could afford the dyed cloth. It is because of this that the color purple became associated with royalty.

Today, Tyre is a city in southern Lebanon, south of Beirut. It is filled with archaeological treasures such as a Roman-Byzantine necropolis and the largest Roman hippodrome ever found.

Zion (zye-uhn)

Itinerary: 2 Samuel 5:6-12

Traveler: David, second king of Israel

Destination: Zion

Topography: Zion or "City of David" first referred to a Jebusite fortress on the southeast hill of Jerusalem. Mount Zion, as the hill came to be called, was shaped like a human footprint and occupied about eight to ten acres. It was separated from the northern hill of Mount Moriah by a lateral valley. The Tyropoeon Valley lay to the west and the Kidron Valley to the east.

Transportation: foot

What to Take: King David marched with his men.

Arrival: 1000 B.C.

Reason for Visit: David was 37 years old when he became king over all of Israel, including Judah. He and his men marched toward the Jebusite fortress in Jerusalem in order to capture the city and take it for Israel. He knew he would have to be clever because the fortress walls were known to be impregnable. David caught the Jebusites off guard by entering the city through a water tunnel. He subdued the inhabitants, took up residence there, and called his home "City of David."

King Hiram of Tyre sent David cedar logs, carpenters and stone masons with which to build a palace fit for a king.

Things to Do: When David brought the Ark of the Covenant to Zion, he established Jerusalem as the religious and political capital of the united kingdoms of Judah and Israel. Although the prophet Nathan did not permit David to build a temple for the ark because of his excessive bloodshed, the honor was later given to his son, Solomon.

Then and Now: The name Zion did not initially refer to the entire city of Jerusalem, but only to the City of David where the king built his palace and citadel. The summit of Mount Moriah, the modern Temple Mount, remained bare long after David captured Zion. That area was still owned by Araunah, the city's former Jebusite king. Eventually, David purchased the hill for 50 shekels of silver and built an altar there. It was not until King Solomon built the first temple at the top of Mount Moriah that the boundary of Zion was moved northward to include the Temple Mount.

The lateral valley which separated the City of David from the

Temple was filled in by Solomon using dirt. The area became known as the "miloh" or "Ophel" and was the site of Solomon's own palace, as well as the burial place of many of the kings of Israel. The modern Zion Gate of Old City Jerusalem is called "Bab el Daoud" by the Arabs or "Gate of David." It faces Mount Zion, which many believe is the final resting place of David, the greatest king in the history of Israel.

An upper room in The Church of St. Mary of Zion is thought to have been the setting of the Last Supper of Jesus and his disciples. Another church on Mount Zion called St. Peter of the Cockcrow may have been built over the site of the courtyard of the house of Caiphas where Peter denied Jesus three times before cockcrow.

Today, the name Zion is used to refer to the whole of Jerusalem as well as heaven.